The Complete Guide
to Fruit Growing

Peter Blackburne-Maze

THE CROWOOD PRESS

First published in 1988 by
The Crowood Press
Ramsbury, Marlborough
Wiltshire SN8 2HR

www.crowood.com

© Peter Blackburne-Maze 1988
Paperback edition 2010

ISBN 978 1 84797 173 9

Line illustrations by Stephen Moore
Colour photographs by the author

Typeset by SR Nova Pvt Ltd., Bangalore, India
Printed in Spain by Graphy Cems

Contents

By the same author:

The Complete Guide to Vegetable Growing

Introduction

Growing fruit in gardens is becoming increasingly popular these days. Not only that, it's also a lot easier. This is not just because the number of people interested in gardening has gone up in leaps and bounds, but because fruit growing itself has changed. Undoubtedly the main reason for this is the enormous advances that have been made in the breeding of new and more reliable varieties. Apples are the principle beneficiary, but raspberries, strawberries and currants (both black and red) have all received their share of new varieties and, to a lesser extent, so have pears, plums, cherries and gooseberries.

A prime reason for the Increased popularity of growing tree fruits is that much smaller trees can now be grown. With gardens decreasing in size, the need for suitably sized trees is vital if they are to be grown at home at all. Fortunately, though not for the same reasons, fruit farmers also demand smaller trees which are easier to manage and the last twenty years or so has seen a remarkable change in both the size of commercial trees and the ways in which they are grown. Gardeners have not been slow to take advantage of this innovation and trees are now available which can actually be grown in large pots, tubs or similar containers, throughout their life. This has been made possible largely by the use of less vigorous rootstocks, the ready-made set of roots on which all fruit trees are grown. Apples, pears, plums and cherries have all benefited from the development of these new rootstocks.

Another, and rather different, factor is the vast increase in the number of garden centres. People are now much more aware that fruit isn't just something that is bought in a sealed plastic bag in a supermarket; you really can grow it at home. They are also far more prepared to spend money on their gardens. The actual growing of the fruit is also easier. Gardeners are becoming more adventurous and have discovered that producing a crop of strawberries is as easy as growing a row of cabbages. This encourages them and they progress to other fruits, which they are finding just as easy to grow.

Equally important is the increasing number of pick-your-own fruit farms. These have come about because of the ever-mounting cost and difficulty of finding experienced fruit pickers. Along with garden centres, these farms are now providing town, as well as country, dwellers with a day's outing and something to show at the end of it. What could be nicer than pleasant and profitable fruit picking in the fresh air of the countryside? This is something that people living in the country tend to forget, or take for granted.

Then again, even if you can't be bothered to do the actual picking yourself, farm-gate sales enable you to buy fruit a great deal fresher and often cheaper than you would otherwise be able to.

All this has led to a predictable increase in the popularity of fresh fruit and a consequent rise in the number of gardeners having a go at growing it themselves. 'You've seen it; you've tasted it; now grow it.' – it's as simple as that. Nor do you need an enormous garden. As has been mentioned, the new and less vigorous varieties and rootstocks have made it possible to grow fruit trees quite easily in ridiculously small spaces.

The type of training often needed by these more intensive tree forms, such as cordons, espaliers and spindles, is clearly something that has to be understood and carried out correctly. However, to most gardeners this is all part of the fascination and joy of gardening. 'Is it going to do what I want it to?'; only the Almighty can answer that but part of the fun is waiting to find out.

Bush fruits, currants and gooseberries in the main, have always been popular garden fruits and different ways of growing some of them (for example gooseberries and red currants as cordons), means that even the smallest garden can now find room for them. Another aspect is the appearance of several new fruits that have not been grown in Britain before. The kiwi fruit, or Chinese gooseberry (*Actinidia*), is a good example. Though far from being an established type of fruit in British gardens, mainly on account of its questionable hardiness, a number of the more ambitious and curious gardeners are giving it a try.

Similarly, grapes are attracting a greater interest now that gardeners are finding that they are perfectly easy to grow and that some varieties can be converted into very acceptable wine. Blueberries and cranberries are also increasingly sold in garden centres.

Two of the main drawbacks of growing your own fruit used to be (a), that the trees were often too large for small gardens, and (b), that an air of mystique was encouraged to form around the subject by the gardeners of the past who worked in the big houses on huge estates. They regarded anything even remotely technical as secret to all but a chosen few. Some of them genuinely believed that there were only two ways of doing things; their way and the wrong way. Now, though, the age of mass communication has put a stop to all the humbug and secrecy. Besides that, we have found much easier and equally effective ways of gardening.

There is no excuse whatever today for pleading ignorance of some slightly off-beat aspect of gardening, such as the summer pruning of cordon pear trees; the answer can be found in most gardening magazines or in the nearest library.

Easier still, you will find most of the answers here along with everything else you need to know to start you off growing fruit successfully and enjoyably at home.

1 The History of Fruit Growing in Britain

When looking at the history of any group of plants, a good place to start is with the botanical angle as it sets the scene nicely.

The first thing to understand is that the modern cultivated fruits have no naturally occurring wild equivalents; they're made up of countless selections and hybrids of originally wild fruits. For example, it is generally accepted that the modern cultivated apple is a descendant of the wild *Malus pumila*. This is a crab apple that is found growing wild in Europe (including Britain) and western Asia as far east as the foothills of the Himalayas. *M. pumila* is extremely variable in the wild. Probably the best selection from the original is the cultivated crab John Downie, while the most likely genetic intruders are probably *M. prunifolia* and *M. silvestris,* our own wild crab apple. Not content with the natural confusion that exists, Man has introduced yet other species into the picture so the apple's family tree is extremely complex. For all these reasons, the accepted botanical name of the modern apple that we buy in the shops and grow at home is *Malus domestica*.

As regards the length of time over which fruits have been used by Man, any theory can be little more than a guess based on a small amount of knowledge and a lot of circumspection. It is fair to assume that fruits, especially apples, have always been an important part of our diet. Originally, it would have been just a matter of gathering wild fruits and eating them when you felt hungry.

In Switzerland, excavations of prehistoric dwellings have shown the remains of what are thought to be dried half-apples. This suggests that the inhabitants had a knowledge of how to store the fruits for out-of-season use. This has two obvious benefits. First, crops can be grown in far larger quantities than are needed for immediate use, knowing that they will not be wasted. Secondly, it allows the surplus to be kept beyond the time when it is available fresh, thus ensuring that the supply of food is maintained.

In Britain we know that fruits have been used since at least Neolithic times (the New Stone Age) as pips and stones have turned up on several archaeological sites.

The selection and development of improved European varieties is thought to have started with civilisations such as the Greeks and Romans who were, culturally, far ahead of us in Britain. The earliest orchards would have consisted of trees raised from pips and, provided that the farmers or gardeners stayed with the original and true species, the seedlings would have continued to come true to type. However, it was when new selections and hybrids came to be used that the trouble started.

Anyone who has grown an apple tree from a pip will have noticed the very same thing that the early fruit growers found; that the offspring were not the same as the parent. It was found that, to propagate a specific variety of fruit successfully, it had to be done by vegetative methods; not by seed. That is as true today as it was all those years ago. With currants, gooseberries, strawberries, cane fruits and so on, propagation is by taking cuttings. However, tree fruits (apples, pears, plums, cherries and so on) are very erratic when attempts are made to strike cuttings.

This discovery in those dark and distant days led to the practice of 'grafting' or 'budding' a portion of the desired variety on to a ready-made set of roots (the rootstock). Whereas grafting involves the use of a short length of shoot containing two or three buds, in budding only an individual bud removed from the parent shoot is used. This discovery was really the turning point in fruit tree production because there was then nothing to prevent the introduction of any number of varieties, knowing that they could be propagated true to type.

This is confirmed by the writings of Romans like Virgil, Cato and Pliny, the last of whom listed some two dozen apple varieties. It is not known if these were the result of deliberate breeding work, but it is more likely that they were either naturally occurring variations or chosen selections. In any event, the outcome was the same; the birth of modern cultivated fruits.

With fruit well established with the Romans, its spread and future was assured. It marched across Europe with the armies, being planted wherever they settled for any length of time, and eventually crossed the Channel into Britain. However; although there is evidence that fruit was in general use by the time the Romans arrived, everything then seems to have become a lot more organised. We still don't know,

though, if it was actually cultivated or simply gathered from semi-wild trees.

With the coming of the Normans, however, all that changed. The arrival of William the Conqueror in 1066 heralded a new era in fruit growing, with intentional and organized growing. Indeed, the monasteries were probably the first places to cultivate fruit in Britain according to a system.

As regards the varieties grown in those days, a few were probably inherited from the Romans, such as the dessert apple Decio, but they would have been few and far between. Most of the true Roman varieties are likely to have been unsuitable for the English climate. Decio is almost certainly the oldest named apple in Britain. It is said to date from around 450 ad and to have been brought over by the Roman general Etio. Once the Normans arrived, French varieties would have been grown as well.

By the end of the thirteenth century, there were some comparatively choice apple varieties; notably the Pearmain and the Costard. The pearmain was the standard dessert apple, with the costard its cooking counterpart. It was still the best cooker and very popular during Shakespeare's time.

In about 1500 Richard Harris, the fruiterer to Henry VIII, brought some apple shoots over from France; amongst them were 'pippins'. The name pippin probably referred to the fact that, unlike others, this particular type of cultivated apple came true from seed. The Golden Pippin, since disappeared, was certainly the best. At last there were the beginnings of a real apple industry in Britain.

One of the greatest names in fruit growing at that time was Thomas Andrew Knight. In the late eighteenth and early nineteenth centuries Knight's breeding work covered most fruits and vegetables. Probably his best-known creation is the cherry

Waterloo; still occasionally grown and one of the best black dessert varieties. Several of the old varieties still exist; not exactly in commercial use but in the variety collections (mainly apples) at the National Fruit Collection at Brogdale Farm, at Faversham in Kent.

Along with the earlier Golden Pippin, the Queening and the Pearmain seem to have been the most popular desserts. Early cooking apples included the Codlin and Pomewater. The Pomewater was popular with apothecaries who used it for making pomade, a sort of Elizabethan 'Brylcreem'. The development of cider varieties was also going on apace.

During Stuart times and the Restoration, a much greater interest was being shown in foreign varieties. John Evelyn was a great champion of the Calville varieties. These are a classic example of French varieties not thriving in England simply because they require a milder climate. The Nonpareil seems to have enjoyed greater success and was widely grown commercially in Kent.

By the end of the seventeenth century, fruit growing was an established industry. However, in spite of all this activity, there was still very little by way of an organized breeding programme; most new apples were chance seedlings found by gardeners on the large country estates. Ribston Pippin, on the other hand, was probably a French seedling that was imported and planted in the gardens of Ribston Hall near Knaresborough in Yorkshire. By the mid-1800s it had become recognised as one of the finest eating apples of all time and it is still listed by most good nurserymen. Another famous apple, Blenheim Orange, was discovered in about 1740 by a Mr Kempster at Woodstock, the nearest town to Blenheim Palace, and the next

milestone occurred in about 1825 when Mr Richard Cox of Colnbrook near Slough bred Cox's Orange Pippin; probably the most famous apple of all time.

The greatest cooker of them all, Bramley's Seedling, also came on the scene about then. Mary Ann Brailsford raised it at Southwell, Nottinghamshire, between 1809 and 1813, although it wasn't made generally available until 1876 by Mr Merryweather, a Southwell nurseryman who was also responsible for the widely grown Merryweather Damson.

Worcester Pearmain was a seedling from Devonshire Quarrenden and was introduced in 1873 by the nurseryman Smith of Worcester. As an early eaten it was the main commercial variety for almost a hundred years, until Discovery came along in the 1960s.

Nothing approaching these in importance appeared until comparatively modern times. Cox and Bramley are still the most popular and widely grown apples in Britain, both commercially and in gardens.

There was, in the nineteenth century, not only an international exchange of ideas but also one between the commercial and private worlds in Britain. The essential difference between the two was, and still is, that in gardens quality was the all-important factor, whereas in commercial orchards it was mainly quantity that mattered. Oddly enough, there is now a drift towards the same type of low cost, low maintenance methods of cultivation in both situations.

This takes us back to the subject of rootstocks because, besides providing the most convenient method of propagation for fruit trees, it is they that are responsible for the ultimate size and cropping of the tree. However, it wasn't until the mid-nineteenth century that anyone tried to regularise the situation and set up an apple rootstock trial. Unfortunately, it wasn't a great success and it fell to East Mailing Research Station in Kent to take on the task, during the First World War of sorting out the chaos. There now exists a complete range of rootstocks for all the major tree fruits. Apples especially have an enormous choice, entirely due to their status as our principal fruit crop.

Indeed, the history of fruit growing in Britain has centred on the apple with other fruits taking second place. Pears, for example, had very much the same background as apples and tended to follow them around. They also started life in Asia Minor and are descended from the wild pear, *Pyrus communis*. Other species have joined them but in nowhere near such a number as *Malus* species went into apples. It is interesting to note, though, that Oriental pears are descended from *Pyrus serotina* and not *P. communis* as are European varieties. Pears were certainly known and grown in southern Europe in Roman times but there is no evidence that they existed in Britain before the Roman occupation. In fact, there appears to have been little enthusiasm for them before Norman times, probably due mainly to their doubtful hardiness. They did not have the injection of toughness that apples derived from *Malus siberica*, the Siberian crab apple. Added to that, the only ones that appeared to grow in Britain were uneatable. They slowly found their way over from France but all those introduced up to and including the thirteenth century were largely cookers rather than dessert.

The first British-bred pear was probably the Warden, but this seems to refer to a type of pear rather than a single variety. It was, or they were, raised at Warden Abbey between Bedford and Biggleswade and was a cooker. Although the Wardens have disappeared, many of the old varieties are still available: the high quality French pear Glou Morceau started life in 1750, while the Jargonelle is probably even older. These pale into insignificance if the history of the Autumn or English Bergamot is to be believed. It is said to have come over with William the Conqueror and could even be the Assyrian pear referred to by the writer Virgil, although this is unlikely.

Just as Cox is the best-known apple, the equivalent pear is probably Williams', or Williams' Bon Chrétien, to give it its full title. In spite of the French name, it is as English as Cox and was raised at Aldermaston in 1770. Questionably the most widely-grown pear came from the Rivers' 'stable' in 1894 – the Conference. The finest pear of them all, Doyenne du Comice, was a true French variety. It was raised in Angers and first fruited in 1849.

Just as the growing of apple trees on different rootstocks revolutionised apple tree production, so did it also affect pears. With them, though, it actually improved or worsened the fruit quality, depending on the type of root-stock. Back in the mid-sixteenth century it was discovered that quince rootstocks were consistently the best, and so it remains to this day.

Domestic plums, *Prunus domestica,* are generally accepted to be descendants of a cross between *P. spinosa* (the sloe) and *P. cerasifera* (the cherry-plum) with an occasional touch of *P. institia* (the bullace) from time to time.

The plum's first appearance in Britain is almost certainly pre-Roman because stones have been found in Late Iron Age settlements. Cherries are much older, the modern sweet (dessert) varieties mostly stem from the wild bird cherry, *Prunus avium,* whilst acid cherries, like the Morello, are descendants of *Prunus cerasus.* The bird cherry is still a native of our woodlands.

The introduction of other tree fruits, and soft fruits such as strawberries and raspberries, really followed along much the same lines. Fossilised remains of strawberries have been found in Cumberland and these are pretty much the same as *Fragaria vesca,* our common wild strawberry. Raspberries, though not fossils, have a similar history. Their seeds have been found in deposits left by glaciers at the end of the last Ice Age. These were certainly of *Rubus idaeus,* the wild raspberry that is still found throughout Britain and, indeed, most temperate zones around the world.

The scene is now set for us to grow for ourselves the results of these years of evolution and development.

2   Different Ways of Growing Fruit

The arrival of new varieties and the ability to buy and grow much smaller and less vigorous fruit trees and bushes has led to many more ways of growing fruit. There still remains, however, the traditional system of growing fruit in the open garden, with conventional sized trees planted in a border or lawn still being the most popular. This is the least complicated system and, although crops may not always be as large for a given area as they are with the more intensive systems, they are rewarding and perfectly adequate for the little work involved in the tree's upkeep.

Suitable types of tree for growing untrained in the garden include the standard, half-standard, bush, dwarf pyramid and spindle.

Where space is limited, or where you would like to have more types and varieties of fruit than would be possible with full-sized trees, one of the intensive methods is needed. Dwarf pyramids can again be included here, but we normally think of intensive methods as referring to cordons, espaliers, fans and other training systems. With all these methods, the trees are trained against wires or canes into rigid branch forms. Pruning in the summer is desirable as well as in the winter.

It is also possible to train some kinds of bush fruits, such as red and white currants and gooseberries, into these shapes. This results in a great saving of space for when they are grown as traditional bushes at least 5ft (1.5m) is needed between each.

Certain fruits can also be grown in a greenhouse. The kinds that usually spring to mind are dessert grapes and possibly peaches and nectarines. However the choicer varieties of fig also need this kind of protection along with, in all but the mildest areas, kiwi fruit (Chinese gooseberry – *Actinidia* species).

Oranges, lemons and grapefruit can also be grown reasonably easily in a heated greenhouse and even bananas and pineapples, though a lot more heat is needed for these and at least 10ft (3m) headroom for bananas.

Unheated greenhouses can also be used to house and protect hardy fruits (apples, pears etc.) growing in pots, or similar containers, when harsh weather threatens in the spring or late summer.

In fact, growing fruit trees and bushes in containers is a separate and distinct branch of fruit growing and one that perhaps presents the greatest challenge of all. By the same token, the satisfaction of doing it right and getting good results more than makes up for the extra work and attention needed.

All these different aspects of fruit growing are covered later, but let us now look at the various tree forms (shapes) that we can use in the garden.

TREE FORMS

We have seen that fruit trees are very seldom raised from cuttings or seed; either a single bud or a small shoot of the required variety is budded or grafted onto a ready-made set of roots called the rootstock. Not only is this the surest way to achieve success but it also enables us to control the vigour and ultimate size of the tree. This is covered in more detail in Chapter 3.

Along with the characteristics of the rootstock, though, has to be considered the vigour of the actual variety that you are thinking of planting. For example, it is very difficult to keep a tree of the cooking apple Bramley's Seedling small because it is a naturally vigorous (strong growing) variety. On the other hand, the eating apple Worcester Pearmain is rather slow growing so it takes a long time to grow into a large tree. Clearly this will have a bearing on the choice of variety for a particular garden.

The benefit of this wide range of vigours and sizes is that it is now possible to buy apple trees that will grow to almost any eventual size. Nor are other fruits excluded from this wide choice, though, admittedly, the scope is more limited.

Standards

The most vigorous and largest fruit tree is called a 'standard'. This has a trunk about

Standard apple trees such as these used to be common in orchards and gardens of the past, but are now far too large for most gardens.

6ft (2m) tall and the actual tree, depending on the type of fruit and the variety, may be 20–30ft (6–9m) high with a similar spread. Cherries, except for the acid Morello type, can grow even larger. Apples, pears, plums and cherries can all be grown as standards but, and it is a big 'but', standards only have a place where there is ample room. Few gardens are large enough for them these days. This great size, of course, is not only awkward because of the space the tree takes up; a tree as large as that is also hard to pick, prune and spray.

When planting standards, allow 18–24ft (5.5–7m) between trees.

Half-Standards

Next down in size, and probably the best tree form for a specimen in a border or lawn, is the 'half-standard'. Although smaller, it still stands 15–20ft (4.5–6m) high on a trunk some 4ft (1.2m) tall. It is this length of trunk, though, that makes it so suitable for gardens; there is ample height to mow or cultivate under without getting tied up

in the branches and there is enough room to grow other plants right up to the base. The same types of fruit that are grown as standards can also be grown as half-standards.

Similar problems to those encountered with standards, as regards size, apply to half-standards but not to the same extent. Plant the trees about 20ft (6m) apart.

Bush Trees

For many years, 'bush' trees have been the most popular both in private gardens and in commercial orchards. They are small in comparison with standards and half-standards and will produce good crops in well under ten years. Bush trees have about 30in (75cm) of trunk, but are still capable of reaching 12–15ft (3.5–4.5m) in height. They are, thus, just smaller versions of the same basic theme.

In a garden, the short trunk might be thought to be an advantage, and in respect of the tree's ultimate height and ease of working it is. However; it is the same short

A half-standard tree, the biggest that can be recommended for all but large gardens.

A bush tree with a trunk of some 2ft (60cm) – a popular tree for orchards and gardens.

trunk that is also the chief disadvantage; it results in a tree whose bottom branches are too low for working under or growing anything beneath and which, if not controlled, will bend down to the ground with the weight of fruit.

Allow 8–18ft (2.5–5.5m) between bush trees, depending on the natural vigour of the tree and the rootstock.

Apples, pears, plums, cherries and, at a pinch, peaches are all suitable for growing in this form. One has to be slightly guarded about peaches because, except in really mild districts, bush trees in the open are too exposed to be completely satisfactory; they do far better when trained against a west or south-west facing wall or fence.

The three tree forms, standard, half-standard and bush, are comparatively easy to prune because they are shaped roughly as Nature intended and no elaborate training system is needed. The snag is that, once they reach a certain size, all will require ladders for picking and pruning. In addition, their height can make them difficult to spray and protect from spring frosts. Given a large enough garden, both bush and half-standards are fine; the actual choice will depend on whether or not you want to use the ground beneath them.

As already mentioned, half-standards make fine specimen trees in a lawn or border, but they can equally well take their place in the vegetable garden, as can bush trees. Two important points that need to be taken into account here are that all trees cast heavy shadows when they are in leaf and that they often need spraying at times when it isn't always desirable for the spray to fall on other plants nearby. This is especially so with vegetables as it frequently happens that they are ready to pick when the trees need to be sprayed.

Spindlebush Trees

Growing spindlebush fruit trees in gardens should be more popular than it is. They are small (no ladders needed); they are easy to grow; they need very little pruning after the first few years and they start cropping early in their life. What more could you want?

A spindlebush tree has a single central stem (a leader) with the branches spreading outwards from this, rather like those of a Christmas tree. This contrasts with the more usual open-centre vase-shape of fruit trees. The crop is carried, initially, on the shoots (laterals) that grow out from the central stem and then on side shoots that develop on these. When branches have been cropping for four or five years, they may need to be shortened or cut out completely to make room for younger and more fruitful ones. Some of the lower branches are allowed to stay for longer.

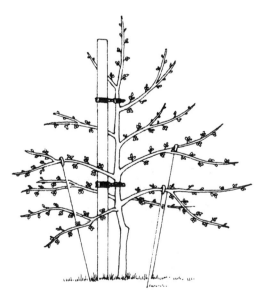

A young spindlebush tree, with its branches tied down to encourage it to fruit.

This is simply because there's nothing below them to be shaded.

Most fruit trees will start cropping earlier and will bear greater crops if they are left judicially alone, as regards pruning. This is the principle of the spindlebush. Where overcrowding occurs higher up the tree, offending shoots are usually cut back to leave a stub an inch or so long that will give rise to one or more future fruiting shoots.

One way of making a fruit tree crop earlier is to tie down its young shoots to below the horizontal. This is because horizontal shoots and branches start fruiting earlier than do vertical shoots, which also carry less fruit. Once new shoots have been tied or weighted down for a year or so, they will stay in place on their own.

Another principle is that fruiting is the most effective way of reducing growth and, once a shoot has started to fruit, it will continue to do so.

To buy an apple or pear tree partly formed into a spindlebush tree is almost impossible, so buy a maiden (one-year-old), preferably with 'feathers'; these are side shoots that grew on the young stem during its first year.

After winter planting, and because we want key branches to grow first and then fruit, four of the strongest are retained. The lowest one should be no less than 60cm (2ft) from the ground. These are all cut back by half to a downward or outward pointing bud. All other feathers are cut back to their point of origin. The central leader is shortened to four or five buds above the top feather and the tree is then tied to a stake.

If the maiden tree is a 'whip' (unfeathered), cut it back after planting to 90cm (3ft) tall. A year later, it will be much the same as a feathered tree and needs to be treated accordingly.

Each winter, the extension growth on the central leader is shortened by a third. Cut to a bud that is pointing in the opposite direction to that in which it was cut the previous winter so that the stem is kept as vertical as possible (if rather zig-zag at this young age). If there are any strong growing shoots coming from the main stem at a narrow angle (they will usually be near the top leader), remove them completely. We want shoots to be growing out as near to right angles to the central stem as possible. Any other new shoots that grow out from the main stem are tied or weighted down to the horizontal in the following winter so that they remain short and fruitful. If any are clearly causing overcrowding, they need to be removed as soon as you see them.

When the first fruits are produced, often in the following year, the growth of the tree will slow down; leading to even more fruit.

The only other pruning, beyond what I have already said, is when the upper branches begin to shade those beneath them. They should then be shortened appropriately or, if this doesn't cure the problem, they need to be cut out. Similarly, fruiting side shoots on the lower branches are cut out when the quality and/or quantity of their fruit deteriorates.

Once the tree has reached a convenient height, which is normally 2–2.5m (7–8ft) tall, upward extension growth is cut out every winter; to leave just the side shoots.

Cordons, Espaliers and Fans

The fruit trees that take up the least space are certainly the various rigidly trained and shaped forms: cordons, espaliers, fans, and their variations. They do, however; have to be trained and tied in to wires to keep them in the right shape and in good order.

They can be grown either against a wall or fence or in the open garden.

All need summer pruning (see page 61), but are very economical of ground space. They should always be grown on a suitably dwarfing rootstock, however. The simplest shape is the cordon; a single stem without any side shoots at all but furnished with short fruiting spurs on which the fruit is borne. Cordons also have the advantage of coming into cropping sooner than most other tree forms.

They are normally grown as oblique cordons at an angle of forty-five degrees. This makes them less vigorous and more fruitful and also allows each tree to be larger but still reach the same height above the ground.

Allow 3ft (1 m) between trees, with 6ft (2m) between rows if grown in the open garden.

Apples and pears are often grown as cordons, but red currants and gooseberries may be as well (although not blackcurrants). In their case, however, it is usual to grow them as vertical cordons with two or more upright 'branches'. Having only one makes it a very expensive job to plant up a row and also means that much of the natural vigour of the bush is wasted, most of the shoots being cut off.

Apple and pear cordons are best pruned only in the summer but the currants and gooseberries need treatment in the winter as well.

An espalier is really a glorified cordon in that, from a vertical central stem, pairs of horizontal branches are trained out at regular intervals, usually 9–12in (23–30cm). These branches are not allowed to form any side-shoots but, like the cordon, the fruit is borne on short fruiting spurs. Espaliers, too, need training wires and may also be grown against a wall or in the open.

Clearly, espaliers take longer than cordons to attain their full size, but far fewer trees are needed for a given length of row. Plant 9–15ft (3–4.5m) apart according to vigour.

While apples and pears are the main fruits grown as espaliers, stone fruit (plums, cherries, peaches etc.) perform better when fan-trained. This is because they are rather susceptible to the disease bacterial canker, which often results in whole branches having to be cut out. Red and white currants and gooseberries may also be grown as fans.

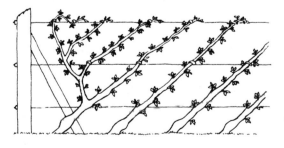

Cordon trees are grown as single stems, except for those at the end of a row which are trained to fill the available space.

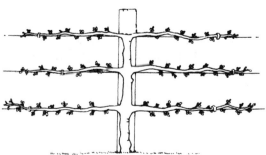

A three-tier espalier.

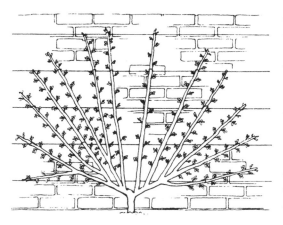

A fan-trained tree against a warm wall. This training method is suitable for all 'stone' fruits, especially peaches.

With fan trees, the branches radiate from a short trunk and, as the 'rays' get further apart, side-shoots are trained out to fill the gaps.

Fruit trees may be grown in various other more complicated and impressive shapes, but those described are the basic ones and, with a little patience, even the most complicated espalier is well within the capabilities of most gardeners.

There is, however; an abhorrence in the commercial fruit growing world of anything that requires work which is as time consuming and as complicated as summer pruning and training. In gardens we aren't burdened to quite the same extent as the fruit farmer with regard to our time; in fact, many of us are quite happy to spend hours pruning. We enjoy it. But there is an understandable move on fruit farms towards minimum-upkeep trees and, for those gardeners with less time or enthusiasm, broadly the same methods are quite easily adapted for use in gardens.

There are, of course, many other shapes in which fruit trees can be grown, but those already described cover most eventualities and are well within the ability of any gardener interested enough to find out about them and carry them out.

An unusual form for use with apples is called the 'compact columnar'. To be accurate, rather than being a system of training it is actually a completely different kind of naturally occurring tree. It started life in Canada as a sport (mutant) on a tree of the variety MacIntosh. Instead of developing in the normal way, one particular branch on the tree grew less vigorously than normal; it was also straight and without side-shoots. The branch was propagated and the resulting trees were given the varietal name Wijcik (pronounced wich-ic), after a local town. By UK standards, Wijcik was a pretty poor quality apple, but the physical characteristics of the trees were so desirable that it was crossed with existing varieties in an effort to produce a new race of apple trees. It is this first generation that is now undergoing trials.

The trees look very much like vertical cordons but, of course, they grow like that without any pruning or training. They have few, if any, side-shoots as most of the buds develop into blossom buds instead of growth. Any which do grow into shoots are pinched out as soon as they are seen.

Clearly, a tree which is going to grow slowly, vertically, without side-shoots and with an abundance of fruit buds is what we are all looking for. However there is very little point in it if the fruit is uneatable.

Those, then, are the various tree shapes and forms that are suitable for private gardeners. You can often buy partially formed trees at nurseries or garden centres (for example, a three-year-old espalier), but, even if these are hard to come by, you will see in Chapter 6 that you can perfectly well form your own.

3   Choosing Kinds and Varieties of Fruit

It may seem that there is so much thinking and considering to be done before you even start, that growing fruit in a garden is a complicated business and almost more bother than it's worth – nothing of the sort.

What we have been talking about up until now and most of what you will read in this chapter are simply the points that will pay for a little thought during the planning stage. What, for instance, is to be gained by planting a tree that could grow to a massive size in a garden that only has room for a cordon? With a little forethought, this sort of inconvenience is easily avoided. The days are past when you more or less had to take potluck with what the nursery could supply you with.

There are very few rules which, if broken, will lead to disaster; these are suggestions and ideas to help you make a success of a fascinating part of gardening.

Types of Fruit

With that word of encouragement, the next thing that has to be decided upon is what kinds of fruit you want to grow and, along with that, which varieties.

It should go without saying that the first consideration is personal preference. Write down all the different kinds of fruit that you would like to grow. Try to put them in their order of importance to

you. Never mind if you know that they will not all be possible, the list can be shortened later but you would kick yourself if you hadn't considered something that was really perfectly easy if only you had thought of it at the time. The best way of making sure that nothing is missed out is to go through the fruit section of a nurseryman's catalogue. It's really exactly the same principle that you would adopt when considering which vegetables to grow. Put them all down and then reject the impossible.

Of course, it's also important to realise that it may be quite easy to grow something that, for the moment, you think a non-starter. That is where this book aims to help you further, by telling you the different 'tricks of the trade' that make miracle-working appear easy.

If, as well as the kinds, you can also make a note of the varieties you fancy, do so; but be flexible because there is a lot more to it than simply likes and dislikes.

Having made a list of the fruits you want, shorten it by eliminating the impossibilities on the grounds of common sense. The first to go are those fruits which would not be hardy enough either for your locality or for your particular garden. Obviously it is impossible to draw a line on a map of the country and say 'below this, yes; above it, no', but there are certain broad limits of hardiness.

19

Figs, grapes, peaches and apricots, for example, can really only be grown safely outdoors in the southern and western parts of the UK.

To this should also be added loganberries, but they are a rather special case. Unless you have a particular reason for wanting them, they are best avoided in the colder areas. The chief reason for this is that there are other hybrid cane fruits, such as the tayberry and the sunberry, which are hardier. They are also heavier cropping and, quite honestly, are likely to spell the end of loganberries all over the country as they are superior to it in every way. If you insist on growing loganberries, choose the thornless type, LY654. This crops as heavily as the thorny one and is said to be slightly hardier.

The main difference between the north and south as regards warmth is not so much the actual temperature as the length of the summer. Pears, for instance, that grow well in the south should always be grown in the warmest position possible when growing them in the north. Against a sunny wall, for instance, they will start growing one or two weeks earlier and carry on a couple of weeks later in the autumn. This makes the summer up to a month longer against a sunny wall than in the open garden. Even within an otherwise favourable area, an individual garden may be so open and exposed to winds that certain types of fruit are impossible to grow. This often occurs on the coast where salt-laden winds are the main problem.

The main objection to growing certain kinds of fruit in the colder districts is that some flower much earlier than others. Clearly this is going to make a lot of difference. No matter how tough the actual wood of a fruit tree or bush is, if it flowers early in the spring, you will run the risk of having the flowers killed by spring frosts. As a rule, the stone fruits (plums, cherries, peaches etc.) are the most likely to be damaged in this way. They can flower as early as March. However, most other tree and bush fruits are also liable to this problem. We will look at ways of reducing the risk later (pages 24–28 and 35–37).

The business of what can safely be grown in a given district, therefore, is far from easily settled, but there are obviously general indications which it is as well to bear in mind when choosing kinds and varieties of fruit On the whole, and with the above exceptions, there is very little to worry about and, if there is still doubt in your mind, consult a local garden centre or someone nearby who knows what they are talking about.

Varieties

This brings us on to varieties because, not only do different fruits vary in their hardiness and in the times at which they flower but so also do varieties of the same fruit. For example, the pear Louise Bonne starts flowering over a week before Comice. Clearly the early flowering varieties should be avoided in frosty and exposed areas.

Once hardiness has been considered, those fruits that have qualified must be submitted to the 'vigour' test. With most tree fruits, it is the rootstock which determines how strong or weak a tree is going to grow. This will tell you not only how fast the tree will grow, but also how much room they will *eventually* occupy. Remember, although a 'standard' tree will start off the same size as a dwarf pyramid, that is where the similarity ends.

With fruit trees, the main consideration is likely to be the type of tree to grow (half-standard, bush, cordon etc.). It may not always be possible to buy locally a tree of your chosen variety on the rootstock you would like. However, you will certainly be able to get it from a specialist fruit nursery, the only difference being that you'll have to wait until the winter for it to be sent. Incidentally, I prefer to buy bare-root plants (available during the winter) to those in containers. On the whole, they transplant better.

With all fruits, the size and vigour of the tree or bush will also depend on the variety.

Closely tied in with the space that a tree will take up is the position in the garden that it is to occupy. Choose a sunny and sheltered spot for the best results; never regard a fruit tree as something that can be planted in any old space that there might be. The chances are that it will not be a success.

More thought is needed when planning for tree fruits than for soft fruit bushes and canes, simply because there is a greater choice and they will live for much longer, but soft fruits still need careful consideration. Luckily, most have their vigorous and weak varieties so it isn't too much trouble to make the choice.

Good examples are the gooseberry Invicta, which is a very strong grower, and the new black currants Ben Sarek and Ben Connan, which is considerably more compact than others. Invicta, therefore, needs more room than other gooseberries and Ben Sarek and Ben Connan less than other black currants. Clearly, these characteristics must be considered before any varieties are chosen.

However, just because a given variety of any kind of fruit may be a strong grower, it doesn't necessarily follow that it has to be rejected. For example, gooseberries and red or white currants can perfectly well be grown as a 'U' cordon. This often makes it possible to grow something that would otherwise be a non-starter.

Except for autumn fruiting raspberries, all cane fruits will need a permanent post and wire support system, but this can be either in the open garden or against a wall or fence. If against something, try to make it a sunny aspect.

Raspberries, both summer and autumn fruiting, are rather a special case. Although they occupy relatively little ground, they form what is in effect a hedge and, thus, will cast a heavy shadow on one or both sides of the row. For this reason they should, whenever possible, be sited at the end of a plot so that the ground on only one side will be shaded. Similarly, and if possible, the rows should run north–south so that they do not cause a permanent shadow.

Although the spacing of tree fruits was discussed in the section on. 'Tree forms' in Chapter 2, that of soft fruit bushes and canes was not. These are dealt with under the individual fruits in Chapter 9.

Strawberries are the easiest of all fruits to accommodate because they take up the least room and are only normally kept for a maximum of three crops. Some, indeed, are best grown for just one crop and then replaced with fresh plants. The most convenient place for them is in the vegetable section but, in fact, you don't even need a garden. They will grow perfectly well in pots or growing-bags, provided that these are placed in a sunny position outdoors. An even more attractive way of growing them is in either purpose-made tower-pots or strawberry barrels; these are available in either wood or terracotta. Growing them in a container also means that they are mobile and can be brought under cover to protect them from spring frosts or simply to advance them.

Besides hardiness and vigour (that is, space required) other factors have to be considered and obviously flavour will come high on the list, if not actually top. This, though, is back to personal preference. While some people would say that the apple Golden Delicious is first rate, others regard it as uneatable.

Another difference in many fruits is that there are cooking, dessert and dual-purpose varieties, though it has to be said that dual-purpose ones are seldom better than mediocre for dessert.

Lastly, as regards variety, and maybe most important of all, is the time at which different ones ripen. Most gardeners like to have a succession of fruit; having everything ready together is not only rather boring but it can, in some instances, lead to waste simply because circumstances may not allow any surplus to be stored. Whether or not this happens will depend entirely on the varieties you choose.

One final tip – if you are in any doubt about the choice of either the fruits or the varieties, play safe and consult a good local nursery.

Sources of Plants

We now come to what is perhaps the most important part of setting up a fruit garden; where to buy the plants from.

Until the arrival of garden centres during the 1960s, the usual way of buying fruit trees and bushes was direct from the nurseryman who actually raised them. Sometimes one might be lucky and be able to buy them from a good local garden shop, along with cane fruits and strawberry plants.

Then everything changed. Gardening became more popular and garden centres sprang up all over the place like mushrooms. A direct result of this was the practice of plants of all sorts being grown and sold in containers. More or less overnight, plants which had hitherto only been available during the winter period as bare-rooted specimens could be bought and planted all the year round. Today, this is how the vast majority of plants are bought and sold.

The obvious benefit to gardeners is that you can now go straight out and buy whatever takes your fancy when you want to. It is a seven-days-a-week business for about 364 days a year. Besides the convenience, plants can now be inspected and chosen from possibly a whole batch and the gardener can see what a particular plant looks like, rather than having to rely on a written or verbal description. In the case of fruit trees and bushes, it is unlikely that you will be able to see the actual fruits; but they are nearly always pictured.

When choosing fruit trees and bushes, there are several things to look out for. For a start, they should be in good health. Any showing obvious signs of invasion by pest or disease, such as greenfly and mildew, should immediately be rejected. There are enough problems without buying any.

If you are buying during the dormant season when the plants are leafless, make sure that the previous season's growth is strong. Weedy little shoots are a clear indication that the plant is suffering and could well be pot-bound, and probably starved as well.

When buying something in a container from a garden centre during the growing season, be sure that the new shoots are strong and healthy and that the leaves are large and of a good colour. Small and pale leaves indicate starvation. This is certainly not impossible to correct but it does mean that other less obvious faults may exist as well.

Trees, in particular, must be of a good shape and, if old enough, should have been regularly pruned. This may sound difficult to see, but anyone can easily spot something that has been neglected.

A good indication of a plant's condition and age is the amount of green lichen and algae that has built up on it. If it is really quite green and on the small side, reject it; it has probably been there for a few years already.

Never be tempted, without some experience, to buy the trees that are carrying the most blossom. They may look attractive and fruitful, but there may be some sinister reason for all the flowers – such as the tree being on the point of dying. In a nutshell, if a fruit tree or soft fruit bush looks right, then it very probably is.

With the exception of raspberries, all cane fruits and strawberries are best when raised and bought in pots or small peat blocks. They cost a little more than bare-rooted plants but, for the sort of quantities that we plant in gardens, it is well worth the extra. Raspberries are normally sold as bare-rooted canes and this is perfectly satisfactory; there is very little to be gained, except time, by buying potted specimens.

The other large source of fruit plants is still the general or specialist nursery. Many have their own garden centre attached to the nursery where some plants are offered for sale in containers all the year round, but their main way of selling is usually by mail and during the dormant period.

Strawberries and cane fruits (except for raspberries) are sold in pots, or something similar, but trees and bushes are normally dug up out of their nursery rows and are only available as bare-rooted plants and during the dormant period (November to March).

The actual plants are often cheaper than they are in a garden centre, but you may have to add on the cost of carriage.

It has to be said that the quality of the plants from these nurseries is usually higher than those from garden centres simply because they have had less handling and the roots are in no way restricted. Nurseries are certainly the places to contact if you want either a type of fruit or a variety that is out of the ordinary. After all, very few garden centres profess to be specialists.

One of the most unlikely places to find fruit trees and bushes for sale must be in the High Street multiple stores. Some of them have been selling garden sundries for many years and one in particular has been strong in the horticultural and agricultural markets for longer than most people care to remember. However, plants are something of a departure for them. Their normal way of selling these is with bare roots wrapped in moss or peat, with the whole plant then packed in polythene. The system is called 'root-wrapped'. This hasn't been carried out by the store itself but by the nursery who raised the plants in the first place.

It is a very seasonal trade, being restricted to the dormant period, and when the plants reach the shops, they are doubtless in excellent condition. Unfortunately, however, it only takes a week or so in the high indoor temperatures that are maintained in the selling areas for them to start into growth. Provided that the plants are bought soon after they reach the shops and, once home, are immediately removed to a much cooler environment, little harm should come to them. They should never, though, be bought in winter once the buds have started to grow out.

Possibly the most risky way of buying plants is through a mail order advertisement in the newspapers as the general quality of the produce still tends to be lower than other outlets; but it is also the cheapest.

Without wishing to overplay the risks of 'buying blind', it must always be borne in mind that there is seldom such a thing as a bargain. If plants are cheap, there is usually a very good reason for it and that reason may make them equally unsuitable for the garden. Size is usually the problem. The cheaper they are, the smaller they often are.

We cannot really leave the subject of acquiring plants without mentioning friends, neighbours and other amateur sources. These can provide a valuable supply of free material and are useful when you want a particular variety which you know someone else has.

There are drawbacks, though, and the main one is certainly the possibility that the material is diseased. The classic example of this is virus-infected raspberry canes. For this reason, one should be very careful when begging, borrowing or stealing fruit plants; or any other plant for that matter.

Apart from raspberry canes, other likely acquisitions are currant and gooseberry bushes and strawberries. All are easily propagated at home and are frequently offered by well-meaning gardeners.

Black currants are often infected with Reversion virus, making them useless, while red currants and gooseberries frequently have mildew. Don't let this put you off buying from amateur sources, but it is as well to know what the snags are and what you should look out for.

Unless there is a very good reason for accepting them, and you know their history, it is much safer to buy new plants from a reputable source. After all, they are going to remain with you for many years so it's

worth making sure that you start off on the right foot.

SITE AND ITS EFFECT

Whether you are considering planting new fruit or simply wish to improve what is already there, the main points that will have to be considered are as follows.

Wind Exposure

If a garden is exposed to the elements, a number of things can be expected to happen; and most of them to the detriment of a fruit crop.

The first problem that is likely to arise is in the spring when the wind is cold and from the north or east. This will have a chilling effect and will discourage pollinating insects from venturing out to do their work. Even if they perform, fertilisation is usually poor when the temperature is low.

If conditions are especially bad, the wind could even be below freezing point, thus creating a wind frost. This doesn't have any harmful effect in the winter when the trees and bushes are dormant, but it can be fatal to blossom in the spring.

During the summer, a windy site is going to be harder to spray effectively than a sheltered one. Not only will the material give poor coverage, but it will also tend to drift onto plants that it might not be wise or convenient to treat. The main victims of this are vegetables that are perhaps ready for eating. A spray that requires a period of, say, a week between its use and when a treated crop is safe to eat can play havoc with the catering if it is allowed to drift.

Later on, the real menace of autumn gales can make a nasty mess of apples and pears in particular. Even if the fruit is not actually blown off the trees, it will very probably be damaged by being rubbed and bruised against twigs.

Slope

Another factor to bear in mind is the slope, if any, of the land; much will depend on its direction and severity. For example, if it is steep and faces north, it will be exposed to cold winds in the spring, thus lessening the chances of successful pollination and fertilisation. At the same time, the whole season will be cooler and, therefore, later.

The strength of the wind, however, is usually less important from that quarter for it is those that come from the opposite direction which are the really strong and damaging ones. In March and September, around the equinoxes, are the times when we are most likely to get a south-westerly gale. In March

these can ruin the pollination and fertilisation of early-flowering trees and in September those carrying fruit can be devastated.

However, a hill can also be a distinct advantage; the most obvious instance is that a south-facing slope warms up quickly in the spring and gives earlier crops. Not only do the sun's rays strike it more directly, but it is sheltered from any cold northerly winds. This can be of particular benefit when growing strawberries.

Much less obvious, but far more important, is the fact that a sloping site will be less likely to be damaged by spring frosts, in susceptible areas. Cold air behaves rather like water and is able to flow downhill if conditions are right. On a sloping site the cold air can move downwards to lower ground and is, therefore, much less likely to cause damage to the blossom.

It isn't always as simple as that though, because, if your garden is at the bottom of a hill or in a valley, it is probably in a frost pocket and, as such, is very susceptible to damage in the spring. In these circumstances, there is some benefit in putting up a wall, fence or hedge along the uphill boundary. This will have the effect of damming the cold air as it flows downhill which may, if the frost is only light, prevent the blossom being frosted.

The same precaution can be taken in a garden that is half-way up a hill, but here it is more important to let cold air flow out at the lowest point rather than prevent it coming in at the top. This is best done by ensuring that there is no solid barrier stretching along the entire lower boundary. If there is, it will hold back the cold air and create its own frost pocket.

In such a situation, try to organise a break in the barrier so that the cold air can flow downwards into someone else's garden!

Shade

Turning to shade, this may not at first appear to be much of a problem and, indeed, it may be that any tall trees are providing shelter from strong winds. However, if they are too close and too tall, they will draw up any trees and bushes, and most other plants, come to that, growing in their shade. Another disadvantage is that neither the fruit nor the shoots will receive enough sun to ripen them properly. This leads to poor fruit quality and fewer fruit buds for the following year. A gardener with this kind of problem would do well to consider an alternative to fruit; certainly dessert varieties would fail to thrive as the sun is needed to create the sugar and bring out the flavour.

Although this may appear to be a formidable list of problems in growing fruit in a particular garden, it must be remembered that most of them can be overcome relatively easily. Even those that are unalterable will seldom rule out fruit completely. It will merely mean that a bit more thought and preparation has to go into the planning stage.

Although there is really very little that one can do to alter the basic characteristics of the site that a garden occupies, there are a number of ways in which we can make it more suitable for gardening. Obviously one cannot change a slope or the direction in which it faces, but damage from winds can be greatly reduced by planting a good hedge on the windward side of the plot. Be careful here, though, that you don't simply create a frost pocket and make matters worse than they already are.

Frost

Curing a frost pocket is not always possible, but the simple act of creating a gap in a hedge or fence at the bottom of the garden, as already mentioned, is often enough to allow cold air to escape. This is sometimes unpopular but usually effective. So you see, there is nearly always something that can be done to improve the situation.

The fact of whether a site is in the town or country will have little effect. The general feeling has always been that the country is a good place to grow fruit in, but this is purely traditional and there is no logical or horticultural reason for it. In fact, towns and cities have two big advantages over the country in this respect. The first is that they are often a degree or two warmer and are thus less susceptible to spring frosts. The other is that there are nearly always other fruit trees close at hand to aid with cross-pollination. We'll hear more about this later (page 35).

A natural frost pocket and, right, one created by planting a thick hedge along the downhill boundary of a garden.

If a hedge forms the lower boundary of your garden, it will prevent cold air from escaping. Correct this by making gaps in it.

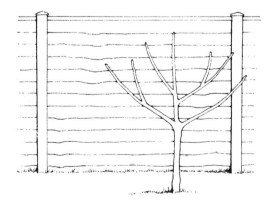

A solid fence makes a good visual barrier but is apt to cause wind turbulence.

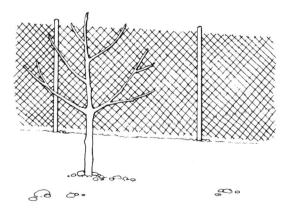

A netting or plastic mesh fence will filter the wind and reduce its speed considerably.

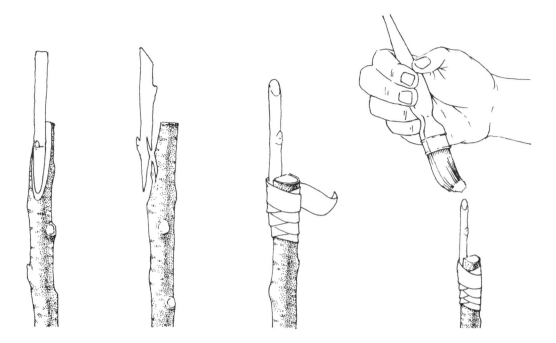

Whip-and-tongue grafting. (Far left and left) The graft (scion) in position. (Right) The scion held firmly in position with raffia or special plastic tape. (Far right) Waxing in the binding and top cut to prevent any drying out of the graft.

However; it was then realised that the root-stocks imparted certain features to the trees that were then grown on them. For instance, a vigorous and strongly growing rootstock gave rise to a similarly behaved tree, while a weak rootstock gave a small tree. This was, and still is, the most important feature of this method of propagation. It enables one to raise any number of identical fruit trees of a known and predetermined character.

The very fact that apples form by far the largest slice of the commercial fruit acreage means that more research has gone into growing them than other fruits. This has led to a wide range of different rootstocks for apples.

Obviously, we as gardeners are going to benefit from all the development work as well, but, luckily, our standard of grow-ing doesn't have to be as high as that of commercial growers. For that reason, the number of different rootstocks used by nurserymen when raising trees for ama-teurs is mercifully small.

Apple Rootstocks

Rootstocks are always described with ref-erence to the vigour. There are three in common use for sale in garden centres.

M9 is normally the most dwarfing one and is useful where a small tree is wanted. These, though, need the support of a stake throughout their life as the root system is small and far from robust. Trees on M9 need good soil if they are to give of their best. It is used for intensive tree forms like cordons, dwarf pyramids and, sometimes, bush trees.

M26 has slightly more vigour and is suitable for small trees on poor soils. Trees should be staked after planting and may need to be always. M26 does not suit all varieties and soils so advice from the nurseryman should be sought. Suitable tree forms are the same as above, with the addition of espaliers.

The most widely used apple rootstock is without a doubt MM106. It is described as semi-dwarfing and is suitable for all garden tree forms and sizes. The only time that it would be inappropriate is for small trees on good soil, when M26 or M9 would be better.

Another rootstock, M27, has appeared on the scene recently. This is very dwarfing and is not normally suitable for gardens unless you are an experienced gardener and know your soil.

Pear Rootstocks

Pear trees are not grown on pear rootstocks but on quince. The choice is limited to Quince A and Quince C. Quince C, however, has had a chequered history and is seldom used now.

Quince A is by far the more common and is certainly the one used by most nurserymen. It produces quite a large tree, but one that is perfectly satisfactory for most gardens and uses.

Plum Rootstocks

Here again, the choice is really between two: the much more common and rather vigorous St Julien A and the newer and smaller Pixy.

Pixy is seldom used now; it had a short and inglorious life because the tree size is not significantly smaller than those on St Julien A, whereas the fruits are. Some nurseries still use it for raising a few Victoria plum trees, but it has little to commend it and nurserymen are unwilling to take up space with another unnecessary rootstock.

St Julien A (but not Pixy) is also used for peaches, nectarines and apricots.

Other Rootstocks

With the arrival of the new and semi-vigorous Colt rootstock, cherries came within the grasp of more home gardeners. However, they are not sufficiently dwarfing to allow cherries to be grown in small gardens.

The main dwarfing rootstocks for this are Gisela 5 and 6. Both are derived from *Prunus cerasus* × *P. canescens*. These two rootstocks are not only dwarfing, but they are also far less susceptible to the two main cherry viruses. They do, though, get phytophthora root rot on wet land.

3ft
(1 metre)

Comparative sizes of apple trees on different rootstocks. (Left to right) M27, M9, M26, MM106, MM111.

Propagating Soft Fruit

'Soft fruit' is the collective term used to cover bush fruits (currants, blueberries and gooseberries), cane fruits (raspberries, blackberries, loganberries, tayberries and the other hybrids) and strawberries. All of them need to be propagated vegetatively to maintain trueness to type, but this can be achieved much more easily than by the budding or grafting needed with trees.

Although all the actual methods are perfectly simple, it is vital that only the most healthy plants are used for propagation purposes if the results are to be what you want. Any that show the slightest hint of disease, either fungus or virus, should be rejected. Bearing this in mind, it will be readily understood that buying ready-made plants from a reliable nursery or garden centre is far and away the safest system to adopt.

Let us assume, though, that all is well and that propagation is about to be undertaken.

Red Currants and Gooseberries

These should be propagated soon after the leaves have fallen in autumn by taking ripe (hardwood) cuttings of the present year's growth. As this is also the time to prune the bushes, the prunings usually make good propagating material.

Cut off the bottom inch or so of curved wood and as much of the top as is necessary to end up with a cutting consisting of 10–12in (25–30cm) of sturdy and ripe growth. As the bushes are going to be grown with a leg (a short trunk), remove all the buds except the top three or four.

Having prepared as many cuttings as you want, make a vertical V-shaped slit in the ground with a spade. Push the cuttings in so that there is about 5in (13cm) between the ground and the lowest retained bud. Firm the cuttings in with your heel.

A year later, either lift the bushes and put them in their final positions or into nursery rows for a further year. In either event, all new shoots are cut back to 2–3in (5–8cm).

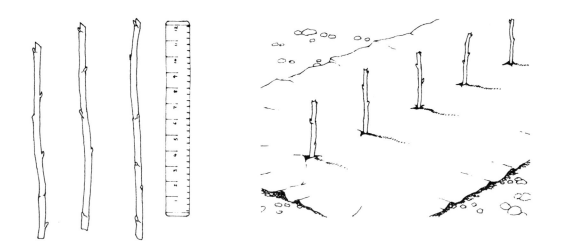

Red currant cuttings with only the top three or four buds remaining. They may be inserted through black polythene to prevent the soil drying out and to smother weeds.

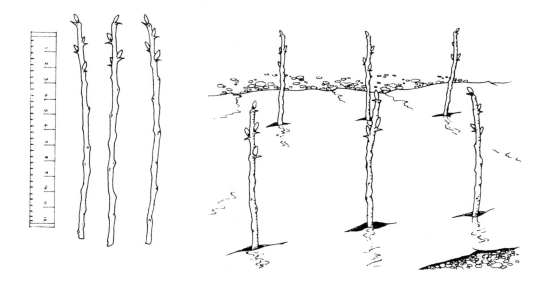

Gooseberry cuttings treated similarly. The best time for rooting these and currant cuttings is in November.

Black Currants

The cuttings are prepared from similar material and in the same way except that all the buds are left intact. The V-shaped slit is also the same, but the cuttings are pushed in so that only the top 2–3in (5–8cm) are showing. This gives a bush with no leg and many of whose branches come from below ground.

A year after inserting the cuttings, they will have good root systems and all growth should be cut back to about 1in (2–3cm). The plants may be lifted then for transplanting but, if you inserted them originally 6–8in (15–20cm) apart, they are best left for a further year, at which time they can be moved to their final places.

This system will quickly give you a strong young bush with plenty of young shoots coming from below ground.

Raspberries

Propagating raspberries is hardly worthy of the term; all that is involved is digging up surplus canes in the early autumn and replanting them as and where required.

There is, though, rather more to it than that because scrupulous care must be taken to avoid any canes that are showing a hint of virus – the scourge of raspberries. Only strong and healthy canes should be used.

The normal practice is to dig up the canes that appear away from the rows. They have to be removed anyway, so why not make use of them?

Immediately after planting the canes, cut them down to 1ft (30cm) to encourage quick establishment and not too many berries in the first year.

Other Cane Fruits

The propagation of these differs from that of raspberries because of their different habit of growth. Whereas raspberry canes are numerous, short and erect, those of blackberries and the hybrids are sparse, but much longer and more supple. This

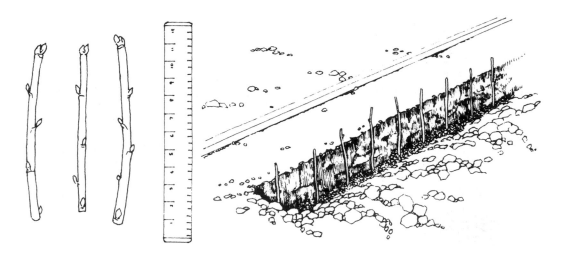

Black currant hardwood cuttings after insertion and waiting for the slit to be filled in.

lends them well to tip layering and, in fact, it often happens naturally if they somewhat neglected.

If your soil is reasonably light, there should be no problems but, if it is heavy, it will need some peat and sand dug in to lighten it.

During July or August, the tip of a new cane is bent down to the ground and inserted into a hole 5–6in (13–15cm) deep. Make the hole sloping towards the parent plant so that the tip lies easily in it. Replace the soil and tread it down lightly so that the tip is held in place. This will root and develop a dormant bud which will grow out either later in the same year or in the following spring.

Always push in a bamboo cane by the layered tip and tie the two together. The tip will not root if it moves and you will also see just where the layered tip is when weeding, cultivating, etc.

Once enough root has formed in the autumn to sustain the tip or new plant through the winter, sever it from the parent, but do not move it until the spring, or even later, to ensure that it is self-supporting.

Strawberries

These are the easiest of all fruits to propagate because they dictate the best method themselves. They have small plants at the end of runners which, if pegged down, will soon form roots and grow into new plants.

They may be pegged down in June or July, as soon as the mini-plants on the runners can be handled. This will ensure strong plants six to eight weeks later which should be planted out before mid-September to give a full crop in the following summer. However, this will often be a nuisance during picking, so I normally delay layering until after I have cleared away the straw, rubbish, etc., after fruiting (see page 101).

If the soil is sufficiently good, the runners can be pegged straight into it, but, if not, sink 3–4in (8–10cm) pots into the ground near the plants and fill them with used seed or potting compost. The runners are then pegged into the compost. This method has the advantage of making the plants mobile when they have rooted so they do not need to be planted straight away.

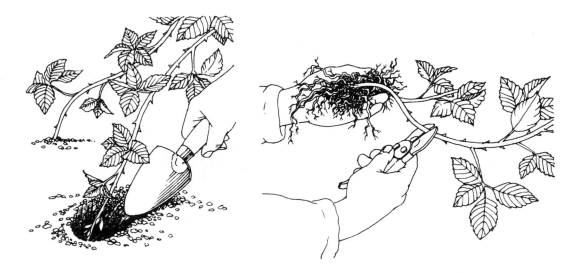

(Left) Tip-layering blackberries and hybrid cane fruits. In July, bury the tip of the current season's shoots. (Right) In the early winter; the rooted tips can be lifted, cut free and planted.

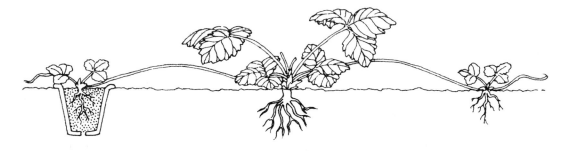

Strawberry runners may be rooted straight into the soil, but rooting them into pots of used potting compost is better.

There we have the main and recognised ways of propagating your own soft fruit plants; be they bushes, canes or strawberries. All are perfectly simple operations, but remember the point about only using healthy parent material; this is the key to success.

POLLINATION AND FERTILISATION

In simple terms, pollination is the transference of pollen from the anthers (the male part) of a flower to the stigma (the female part) of the same or other flowers. It is a prerequisite to fertilisation.

Pollination may be carried out in a number of ways, but, with fruit crops, insect carriers are the most common and efficient. Of these, the honey-bee is by far the most important. Bees, and many other insects, spend most of their active life visiting flowers in search of nectar and, in doing so, become dusted with pollen grains from the anthers. The pollen is then transferred quite automatically to the stigma of the same flower and to that of others as the insect moves on.

Once a pollen grain has reached a receptive stigma, given the right conditions it will germinate in just the same way as a seed germinates. The 'root' of the pollen grain (the pollen tube) grows down through the style and, all being well, reaches and penetrates the ovary. That is the process of fertilisation.

Although the two activities are obviously and closely linked, they are quite separate and it is therefore possible for pollination to occur without fertilisation following; though, clearly, not the reverse.

The conditions necessary for pollination are mercifully similar to those required for fertilisation. The temperature has to be well above freezing (at least above 40°F/5°C) and the atmosphere should be moist. If it is too cold, the pollinating insects will fail to venture out. If the air is too dry, the pollen will not be released and the stigmas will be unreceptive.

As regards fertilisation; if the temperature is too low, the pollen will not germinate, nor will the pollen tube develop.

The question of temperature can be carried a stage further because the time of year when most of our fruit crops flower is also the season when night frosts often occur. These can have a devastating effect and may completely wipe out a fruit crop for that year by killing the flowers. This is why earlier-flowering fruits, like peaches, apricots and even plums, are unreliable in some parts of the UK, unless they are given protection.

Even the earlier-flowering varieties of many other fruits are susceptible to damage. Probably the only safe ones are the cane fruits (raspberries, blackberries etc.); they flower after the frosts are over.

Hand pollination of a peach tree under glass. Use a piece of cotton wool or an artist's soft brush to transfer the pollen from the anthers to the stigma.

Little can be done for large fruit trees by way of protection from frost, but small types, young trees and all soft fruits can be adequately protected from spring frosts simply by throwing some fleece or some polythene over them when a frost is likely. Even the netting used in a fruit cage will often keep in sufficient warm air to prevent the temperature dropping too low. If you are using fleece or polythene, though, be sure to take it off the following morning or you will simply prevent the pollinating insects from reaching the flowers!

The danger signs that should alert one to the likelihood of a frost are plain enough; the days are still and sunny and the nights calm and cloudless. When these conditions occur in April and May, beware.

The object of covering the trees etc. is simple; it prevents the warm air next to the ground from rising and disappearing into the wide black yonder.

The state that the underlying ground is in will also influence the degree of damage that an air frost can do. The whole object of the exercise is to help the ground release its warmth and yet to prevent that warmed air from vanishing upwards. Rough ground, therefore, will release more heat than raked ground or grass, simply because of its greater surface area.

Another aspect of pollination and fertilisation that has to be considered is the fact that all tree fruits carry heavier crops when pollinated by another variety of the same fruit. This is called cross-pollination and, in order for it to be successful, the two varieties must be physiologically compatible (most are). They must also have a good overlap of flowering periods.

Although provision for cross-pollination should, if necessary, be made when planting new trees, the lack of a suitable and nearby pollinator is also a possible reason why existing trees are not cropping as well as they should. We have touched on this before, but gardeners in towns are likely to be better off than those in the country as regards suitable cross-pollinating varieties. This is because there is a far greater chance of another tree of the same kind being in the smaller and closer-surrounding gardens and thus providing different and compatible pollen. Any suitable tree within 100 yards should be adequate.

However, important though cross-pollination is, a lack of it is seldom the sole reason for poor fruit crops; the cause is much more likely to lie elsewhere.

Low temperatures are probably the main cause and there's very little that can be done about that; unless, of course, they are brought about by night frosts.

Cool winds may also lower the temperature sufficiently to keep most pollinating insects tucked up indoors; that is, except the extremely tough and hard-working bumble bee. Clearly, the provision of shelter from cooling winds is going to be beneficial where they exist.

The overlapping of blossom periods is also important. There's very little point in having two varieties side by side if their blossom periods only overlap by a couple of days or so. If the weather is filthy during the overlap, very little pollination will take place.

Find out from the place where you buy the trees if your choice is good from the cross-pollination angle.

37

4 Planning, Planting and Aftercare

PREPARATIONS AND PLANTING

When preparing a site for planting fruit, remember that, except for strawberries, you should be thinking in terms of a useful life of at least twelve years. This applies for even the shortest lived plants, which are normally raspberries. Currant and gooseberry bushes can, if looked after, live for a good fifteen years and tree fruits for upwards of twenty.

With trees, in fact, forty years and more is quite possible, but you might run into the problem of their growing too big and there is always the likelihood that they will be neglected if this occurs. Added to that, old trees will usually need rather better looking after than those in the prime of life. Bearing this in mind, it is easy to appreciate that preparing the soil for planting is an important job; if anything is omitted at this stage, there is very little opportunity of putting it right after planting has taken place.

Preparing the Ground

As a general rule, if plants are to be closer than about 4ft (1.2m) apart, then it is good practice to prepare the ground over all. That is, the whole of the area to be occupied by the fruit should be prepared, not just the planting positions. If the spacing is to be wider than that, just the planting position can be prepared. Even so, for a tree this should never be an area of less than one yard (1 metre) square.

Rather more important than the actual surface area is the depth to which cultivations should go. This is with a view to correcting any compaction or fault in the drainage. One should work on the basis of moving the soil a good 2ft (60cm) deep. This will usually extend into the subsoil and care should be taken not to mix too much of this with the more fertile topsoil. Where the subsoil is chalk, this is especially important, bearing in mind what has been said about the effect of too chalky a soil and its effect on the availability of certain plant foods.

Where just the planting position is being prepared for trees or bushes, the best way of working to this sort of depth is first to dig out the top layer, or spit, with a spade and lay the soil to one side. Then, loosen below this with a fork before returning the top spit. It is a modified form of double digging which, of course, is the best way of tackling a complete patch of land.

Plenty of bulky organic matter, such as garden compost, should be incorporated into both layers. Mixing it well in is important because, if the compost etc. is allowed to remain in layers beneath the surface, the roots will tend to operate only in that area, it being the line of least resistance. This may not appear to matter, but it means that the roots are not making the best use of the available soil and the trees or bushes will tend to be poorly anchored.

Even strawberries need this treatment, although not from the point of view of support. If you want the best from them, bearing in mind that the life of the plants is up to three or four years, then nothing should be skimped. They are fussy plants and need the best conditions if they are to flourish and crop well.

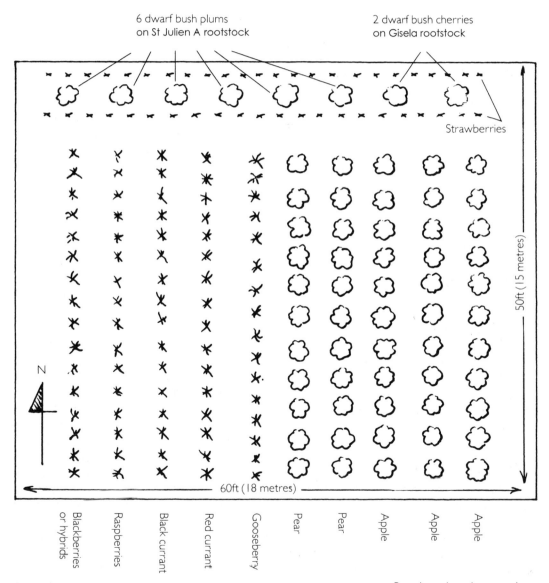

6 dwarf bush plums on St Julien A rootstock

2 dwarf bush cherries on Gisela rootstock

Strawberries

50ft (15 metres)

60ft (18 metres)

N

Blackberries or hybrids
Raspberries
Black currant
Red currant
Gooseberry
Pear
Pear
Apple
Apple
Apple

Adjust numbers to suit your garden; see page 116 for planting distances.

Based on plans drawn up by the Royal Horticultural Society

The importance of good drainage cannot be overstressed. No fruit plant likes to have its roots sitting in water and will quickly show its displeasure if forced into this situation. If roots are not able to penetrate and work to at least 18in (45cm) deep, with 2ft (60cm) for trees, the crops will suffer. Added to that, if the subsoil is poorly drained, there is a risk that the water level will rise into the topsoil during the winter. The bulky organic matter will open up heavy soils so that there is little chance of poor drainage.

These deep workings should be carried out as far in advance of planting as is sensibly possible. This gives the soil time to settle naturally. The trouble here is that, if the soil sinks down too much after planting, you can run into the situation of the whole rootstock being buried and the main variety sending out roots that will soon dominate the rootstock. In any event, try to avoid leaving the deep work until planting time.

Marking Out

Once the soil has been made ready for planting, mark out exactly where the trees etc. are to go.

Strawberries and raspberries will be planted in rows in the open garden so run a line along the proposed row and mark off the position of each individual plant with sticks. The actual planting distances are given in Chapter 9, in the sections dealing with the different fruits, and in the Appendix.

Roughly the same routine is followed with both bushes and trees except that there is less likely to be room for rows in small gardens. Their positioning is just as important, though, and you must make sure that they are given adequate space. Mark their exact position with a cane.

The next job to be done will vary with the kind of fruit and the tree form.

Supports

Anything requiring a post and wire support system should have that put in place before planting. This will include raspberries, blackberries and other cane fruits, cordon and espalier apples and pears and fan-trained peaches. Raspberries will be in the open garden, but the trained trees could be either in the open or against a wall or fence.

Details of the wiring systems will be found under the individual fruits in Chapter 9.

It is safe to assume that most trees will need staking for at least their first few years to encourage them to become firm and established. This will cover all standards, half-standards and bush trees. Dwarf apple trees on M27 or M9 rootstocks will also need staking, usually for their whole life. So will spindlebush trees.

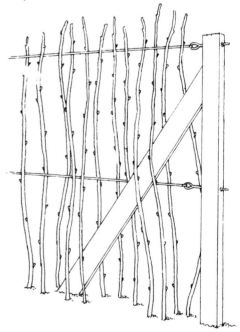

Summer fruiting raspberries need the support of wires fixed at 2ft (60cm) and 4–5ft (1.2–1.5m) above the ground, depending on their vigour.

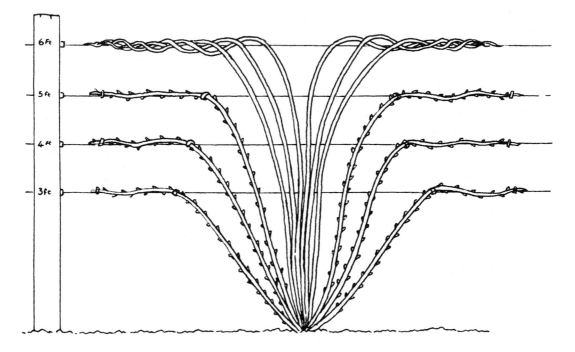

Training blackberries and hybrid cane fruits. The new growth is trained up the centre with the fruiting canes on either side.

The stake should be driven into the bottom of the planting hole before the tree is put in so that it will be on the windward side of the tree. In most districts this means that the stake will be to the west of the tree.

Then plant the tree beside the stake and afterwards secure it with a proper tie. Never drive the stake in beside an already planted tree; this can damage both the roots and the young shoots or branches.

Planting

With most of the preparatory work done, planting can go ahead. Strawberries will normally be in little peat cubes or small pots and can be planted with a trowel. The centre (crown) should just be visible after firming the plant in. As the summer fruiting

varieties should be planted during the period from late July to mid-September, it is particularly important that they are planted firmly and kept well watered to prevent them drying out.

Plant strawberries with the crown of the plant just clear of the soil.

All trees and other fruit plants should be properly firmed in so that the plant is held steady and so that the roots start growing right away.

Raspberries will normally be bare rooted and can be planted simply by making a slit with a spade in the planting position. Place the roots in the slit so that, after firming them in with your heel, the buds at the base of the cane are just below ground.

Other cane fruits should normally be in pots when you buy them. If these are clay or plastic, they must be removed before planting, but those made of peat or bitumenised paper can be left in place; this prevents disturbing the root system and makes for quicker establishment.

Aim to plant cane fruits fractionally deeper than they were previously. This is usually quite easy to see because the planting depth of a bare-rooted plant is shown by a soil ring around the stem.

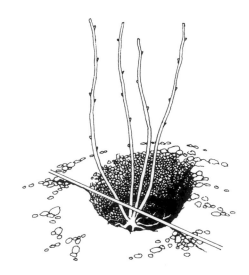

Black currants should be planted with the base of the shoots buried about 1in (2.5cm) deep.

Use a straight stick to establish the depth at which to plant the tree. The soil should be well below the union, the point of budding or grafting.

Red currants and gooseberries must be planted with the lowest branches 5–6in (13–15cm) above the ground.

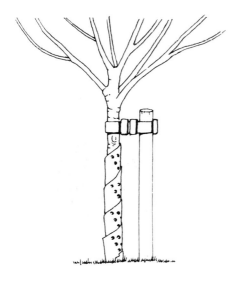

A single vertical stake supporting a tree. Note also the spiral rabbit guard.

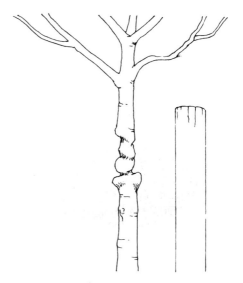

An angled stake is stronger in windy districts. Place the stake downwind of the tree.

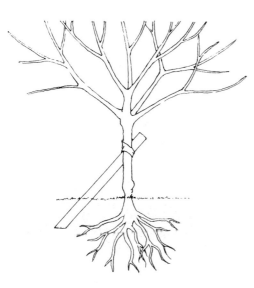

A useful way of supporting larger trees. Two stalks are stronger than one and can be driven into place when the tree is older without fear of damaging the roots.

The result of neglecting a tie.

43

Cordon apples and pears should be planted at an angle of forty-five degrees with the scion (the trunk part as opposed to the rootstock) on top. Remember that you will have to offset the planting hole in relation to the positioning cane to allow for the angled planting.

Trees that are to be trained to a wall or fence should be planted about 9in (23cm) out and leaning towards it.

After planting, the ground should be tidied up to remove footmarks etc. and all fruits except strawberries will benefit from a mulch of garden compost. This helps the soil to retain moisture during the first all-important summer.

When planting in the late autumn or winter, mix in a little bone meal with the planting soil. The phosphates in it will help new roots to develop and the tree to establish before the hard weather.

The actual planting is simple enough but, as with most jobs, there is a right way and a wrong way of doing it. When planting pot- or container-grown plants, unless there is evidence of root restriction, disturb the rootball as little as possible. Simply stand the tree etc. in the bottom of the hole, which must be of the correct depth, and shovel the earth back round it. Do this a bit at a time and tread down the soil as the hole fills up. This should bring it to the right depth by the time all the soil has gone back.

If the tree is badly pot-bound, the outside roots will need to be teased away from the solid ball or they will tend to remain confined and won't spread out.

When planting bare-rooted stock, first spread the roots out in the bottom of the hole and then fill it up gradually with the soil. Tread down the soil every so often and, after the first few shovels have been returned, joggle the tree or bush up and down. This ensures that the soil falls between all the roots and none are left high and dry in air pockets.

If planting in the late winter or during the growing season, though, a general fertiliser like 'Growmore', or the wholly organic blood, fish and bone, should be applied after planting instead of bone meal. This will do much more good as it provides the young plants with the three main nutrients that they require: nitrogen, phosphates and potash.

SOIL MANAGEMENT

Although this may sound rather frightening and technical to new gardeners, it is really just a term that covers all the various things that we do to the soil in our gardens to make it easier to cultivate and, therefore, better for growing plants in.

We have already come across some of the jobs that have to be carried out in connection with growing fruit, but a rudimentary knowledge of the whys and wherefores helps one to understand the purpose of a particular task.

The basic way of tilling the soil is digging; this has many purposes. First, it increases the depth of soil to which roots can easily penetrate. It breaks up the ground so that air can reach down to the roots and surplus water can drain away. Both these features are important if the trees and bushes are to flourish.

Next, digging is the simplest and quickest means at our disposal for incorporating bulky organic matter into the ground. Organic matter is an essential part of all soils.

Those are the main reasons for digging as far as fruit growing is concerned. You can either 'single dig' or 'double dig'.

Double digging is the best way of breaking up the soil to a good depth – about 2ft

(60cm) – and should always be carried out before planting any fruit crop, even strawberries. Once plants are in place, double digging does more harm than good by disturbing and breaking the roots. Double digging involves digging the top spit (layer) with a spade and the bottom spit usually with a fork.

Single digging is what might be called 'ordinary' digging. It extends to one spade's depth and is the routine cultivation that we use to correct soil compaction and to destroy weeds.

For cultivating the soil near to growing fruit plants, the safest tool to use is a hoe. This will move the soil to a maximum depth of about 6in (15cm), but normally only an inch or so. Hoeing is the usual non-chemical method of controlling weeds amongst plants, but it is also useful for breaking up a surface crust which may form after prolonged and heavy rain.

Manures and Fertilisers

Once the trees etc. are in position, the main task is to maintain the level of plant nutrients in the soil. To do this, we apply fertilisers.

Under normal conditions, an annual dressing of a general and balanced granular fertiliser, such as the time-honoured and excellent 'Growmore', is all that is needed. It must be applied at such a time in the winter or early spring as will allow it to dissolve and seep down into the main root zone before growth starts. In practical terms, this means soon after Christmas for large trees (those that require a ladder), early February for medium-sized trees this (those only needing a pair of steps) and early March for more or less everything else.

Strawberries are the exception. If one were to feed them solely in the spring, it would lead to an explosion of growth and leaves like rhubarb at the expense of fruit. The best time to feed them is in July after fruiting. This will build them up for the winter and the following year's crop.

All fertilisers must be applied to the whole root zone of the plant in question, not just the ground in its immediate vicinity. You can ensure this by treating the ground covered by the spread of the branches. They must be applied exactly as directed and, most importantly, evenly. The idea amongst some gardeners that it's sufficient simply to throw a handful at the base of the trunk and hope for the best is a complete waste of time and fertilizer. It may also be extremely damaging because it applies a far greater than recommended amount of fertiliser to a very small area, which can easily scorch nearby roots.

Occasionally, trees and bushes will take a knock in the winter and be rather sluggish to start growing in the spring; this is especially so with those that have only just been planted. If this happens, or if the early foliage is a poor colour, a seaweed extract should be applied as a foliar feed. Spray it on two or three times at fortnightly intervals as soon as you suspect trouble, or even just as an insurance. The results are often spectacular. This is just the same treatment that is recommended for mineral deficiencies.

Another practice that is closely related to feeding plants is the one of mulching the ground beneath them with some form of bulky organic matter. The term 'mulching' simply means that a layer of the material, up to about 4–6in (10–15cm) thick, is spread on the ground.

The main reason for mulching is that it conserves moisture in the upper soil, where the main feeding roots are, by preventing its evaporation. This is especially valuable in areas of low rainfall or where the soil is light or sandy.

A mulch is also a good way of keeping weeds down by smothering out the seedlings before they reach the surface. It won't, though, have much effect on perennial weeds like docks, thistles and ground elder. These should always be killed before mulching or they will benefit from it as much as the crop.

A mulch also adds valuable organic matter to the ground and it is the only completely harmless way of doing this after the trees etc. have been planted. The worms and other creatures in the soil draw it down. It also supplies a limited amount of plant foods.

The material most commonly used for mulching, and as good as any, is well-rotted garden compost. Farmyard manure is equally good but, contrary to popular belief, is seldom better or richer in plant foods. Possibly the smell and origin of manure make one think that it has to be superior.

The greater the area that can be mulched around a tree, bush or canes, the better. With young trees and bushes, though, the mulch should be pulled an inch or so away from the base because mice like to nest in it and feed on the tender bark at the base of the trunk or shoots if given a chance.

An important point to remember about mulching is that it should be applied in March or April when the soil is still thoroughly moist but has begun to warm up a bit. If application is delayed, it could have the effect of preventing rain from penetrating into an already drying soil. If too early, it can keep the soil cold for longer. This isn't particularly important, but it's worth bearing in mind.

This leads us neatly into the final part of this section on soil.

Watering

This is normally thought of as something only applicable to flowers and vegetables, but, because fruit plants carry a crop in just the same way as vegetables, water is equally vital to them.

Fruit trees and bushes are obviously at a distinct advantage over smaller plants because their roots are able to penetrate deeper into the ground and further away in search of water. However, this will only happen if the ground is sufficiently broken up and is not itself waterlogged; hence the need for the deep cultivations before planting.

The crucial time of year when water is required by all fruits is during the growing season from about April to September. However, in the vast majority of gardens, even those in dry areas, there is enough water in the ground to make the irrigation of fruit trees unnecessary; that is except in their first few years when the root system is still shallow and developing.

For bush and cane fruits, the situation is rather different as their root systems are considerably smaller and shallower than those of trees.

Black currants are especially susceptible to water shortage. They need a great deal of water if they are to carry good crops and grow vigorously at the same time.

Raspberries are also thirsty plants. Not only do they have to support the fruit, but they produce all the replacement canes as well. As if this were not enough, their root systems are unusually shallow.

Strawberries need plenty of water as well. They have comparatively small root systems, but they carry fantastic crops in comparison to the weight of the rest of the plant.

It would be rewarding for the ordinary gardener to be able to calculate when and how much water should be applied to a particular crop, but this is really expecting too much, A good habit to get into, though, is to judge the need for watering fruit by observing other plants. When, for example, herbaceous plants begin to wilt and show signs of distress, you can be sure that the fruit is also beginning to suffer and that it is time to water. You must avoid waiting until it's too late before doing anything. Once the leaves and shoots begin to droop and the fruit starts to drop off, you have had it.

Equally important is that, when watering, you should give plenty and that, like the fertilizer, water is applied to the full root zone.

As with watering other plants, aim to give about an inch (2.5cm) at a time; much less than this is pointless because it will be gone before it has had time to soak down to the roots and benefit the plants. One way of estimating the amount you have given when using a sprinkler (the only sensible way), is to place empty tins or jars all over the area being watered and to keep the sprinkler going until there's about an inch (2.5cm) in the bottom of each.

A more accurate and sophisticated way is to buy a metering device that meters out mains water by quantity, so, knowing what area your sprinkler covers, you can calculate how many gallons will be needed for an inch over the whole area. Hozelock have an enormous range of watering gadgets.

One final point on soil management – it is the soil that is entirely responsible for sustaining the fruit plants; they rely on it for nutrients and for water. If it is looked after, plants will be healthy and crops large. If it is neglected, the whole operation will be a waste of time and land.

5   Pest, Disease and Weed Control

What with all the other difficulties that beset us, it will come as no surprise to you to learn that fruit crops are just as susceptible to pests and diseases as are other garden plants. There are pests which eat the leaves, pests which eat the fruit and others which have no particular preference.

Much the same goes for diseases except that, with these, they may be caused by either a fungus or a virus. There are even disorders which are neither fungal nor viral but physiological in origin.

Having said all that and probably thoroughly discouraged you, always remember that only a fraction of the problems that can strike actually do. Many gardeners go through life being completely untroubled by most of them. However, it would be unrealistic and far from helpful if the subject was not covered here because it is an integral part of good gardening.

However, the situation as regards pest, disease and weed control chemicals is extremely fluid, with existing and new materials coming and going so fast that it would be foolish to give any actual recommendations as to which chemical to use for controlling what. There is, though, a very simple and fool-proof way of covering this and that is to go to your local retailer (shop or garden centre) and ask what they recommend for controlling this, that and the other. Much the same goes for the disposal of surplus diluted sprays and undiluted concentrates.

In this case a phone call to your local council should sort things out for you.

Prevention of Pests and Diseases

The main point to realise about pest and disease control is that prevention is infinitely better than cure. It is a more effective method of control, it is cheaper, it prevents damage being done to plants and it greatly reduces the amount of chemical needed.

The purest form of control is what is termed 'managerial' control – the prevention, or dissuasion, of pests and diseases simply by gardening well. The most important part of this is to ensure that the plants have the best possible growing conditions. Strong trees and bushes are much less likely to be attacked and, if they are, they stand a much better chance of coming through the attack with flying colours. An already weak specimen is likely to suffer far more.

Creating these good growing conditions has many facets, including a fertile soil, a good supply of water and plant foods, the correct spacing of the plants, the right kind of pruning and sufficient shelter to protect the plants from extremes of weather. Conditions that are going to encourage pests and diseases must clearly be avoided. Here again we find that correct spacing is important so that the atmosphere is mobile the whole time and less likely to attract fungus spores. This is also a good reason for pruning properly so that trees and bushes are not a mass of crowded and twisted branches. Pruning also covers the removal of dead and diseased branches. If these are allowed to remain, infection can spread to hitherto healthy parts.

General hygiene throughout the garden is vital. A typical example of this is fallen brassica leaves in the vegetable plot harbouring slugs and snails.

With fruit as well, it is not only the fallen leaves but also the fallen fruit that can be carrying pests and diseases. Codling moth caterpillars live in fallen apples and the disease apple scab overwinters on fallen leaves.

Pay great attention to garden hygiene because it can make the difference between winning and losing the battle.

Although the next category is less applicable to fruit than to other plants, the question of alternative host plants must not be overlooked. This refers to the habit of some pests and diseases of living on other plants as well as on fruit. Many greenfly do this, for instance. Always, therefore, keep a watch for trouble on neighbouring trees and shrubs because it could well be that some 'nasty' is lurking there ready to pounce on an unsuspecting apple or pear tree. There's no need to be paranoid about this, but don't forget the possibility and take action if the situation warrants it.

Crop rotation is another aspect that one seldom considers in relation to fruit but it is worth noting that there is a problem called 'replant disease'. This makes it difficult for fruit trees of one sort to flourish in the same spot that was previously occupied by another tree of the same sort. In other words, unless you are prepared

to replace about a cubic yard of soil, avoid planting an apple tree in the same place as one that has just been pulled out.

Yet another help is the use of resistant varieties – those which are unlikely to, or will not, suffer from a specific pest or disease. Virtually all recently-bred raspberries are resistant to certain greenfly and, as it is these insects which spread the extremely common virus diseases, it is clearly in our interest to grow them.

These measures will greatly reduce the number of pests and diseases but certainly you will often be faced with the job of having to beat off an attack by some other means, no matter how many precautions are taken.

Considering the garden as a whole, there are several remedies that can be adopted which don't involve the use of chemicals, such as cardboard collars around brassica transplants to deter cabbage root fly. In the fruit world, the best known gadget is the grease-band. Greasebands are easily bought in gardening shops and are really just a variation on the flypaper theme. They are wrapped around the trunk of fruit trees at about waist height where they will trap several kinds of crawling pest as the creatures pass up and down the trunk.

You can also buy codling moth traps but these are seldom effective enough to do away with the need to spray. However, they do show when the adult moths are present and, therefore, laying eggs. Spraying should then take place.

Obviously, the less we use chemicals, the better. However, if the alternative to chemical control in a particular case is only partially effective, then it is pointless using it. It would be far better to overcome the pest or disease quickly and efficiently with a single application of chemical.

Chemical Sprays

Unlike the treatment of other plants, where there are several alternatives, that of fruit trees, bushes etc. involves almost entirely the use of sprays. This makes life a lot easier in the garden centre or shop when choosing what to buy because all you need concern yourself with are the concentrated liquids and wettable powders, both of which are added to water before application. Forget the puffer packs, the aerosols and the smokes where fruit is concerned.

The basic kinds of spray are fungicides, for killing fungus diseases, and insecticides, for killing insect pests. These two are divided into either 'contact' or 'systemic'.

A contact chemical is one that has to come into direct contact with the pest or disease to kill it. It can do this either by the spray landing on the pest or the diseased surface or by the pest or fungus spores landing on a treated leaf or fruit.

A systemic chemical works differently. It usually has some contact effect, but its main mode of action is to enter the plant that it lands on and, in most cases, pass into the sap stream. In this way, it can permeate throughout the plant and, at the same time, it will be

Harmless and beneficial insects. Ants are largely harmless to fruit and only indicate the presence of greenfly. Hoverflies and ladybirds feed on greenfly. Bumble bees carry out essential pollination.

weatherproof. For as long as the chemical remains active, any susceptible pest or disease landing on a treated plant will perish if it tries to eat or penetrate that plant.

Once it has been decided that spraying is needed to beat whatever it is, the 'nasty' must be identified reasonably accurately so that the correct spray can be bought. It is obviously a waste of time and money to spray 'blind' and hope for the best.

The first point of enquiry is the staff at your garden centre or shop. Several produce excellent 'rogues gallery' charts with the control measures given alongside the problem. Fortunately, however; many sprays today will kill several pests or diseases so it is not always necessary to pinpoint the problem. The more you can narrow it down, though, the better it is because you may find that you can use one of the increasing number of sprays that are only lethal to a small number of pests, or even just one. Clearly, it is these materials that are going to have the least damaging effect on harmless and beneficial creatures.

Having chosen the right spray for the job, read and understand the instructions before you go any further. Take note of precautions, including any fruits that should not be treated, and understand the dilution rates.

When you come to spray, make sure that you do it thoroughly so that every part of the plant is treated; most sprays work on the basis of forming a toxic layer on the leaves and fruit. If this is incomplete, so will the control be.

Avoid spraying in windy weather because this will carry the spray to where it is not wanted; such as next door. In addition, be sure that any vegetables in the vicinity of the fruit are either not yet mature, that they are covered during the spraying or that they will actually benefit from a dose.

In summer, always spray in the evening when the majority of bees and other 'goodies' have retired for the night. Never use an insecticide during the blossom period; all, with the rare exception of one or two, are lethal to bees. Even some fungicides are harmful so it is much better not to spray at all until the flowers have fallen.

When you have finished spraying, dispose of any surplus safely. The best way is to offer it to a neighbour; you then also know that the particular pest or disease is unlikely to attack you again from his direction. Failing that, pour the surplus either onto a piece of empty ground or down the lavatory. Either way it will be so diluted as to be completely harmless.

Any concentrates that you want to dispose of can be flushed down the lavatory; powders may also be wrapped and put in the dustbin, along with empty containers.

Most of these precautions are a matter of common sense and really, can apply to the whole subject of pest and disease control. Do all that you reasonably can to keep trouble at arm's length, but, if this fails (as it often will), use chemicals sensibly. They are a boon to gardeners for doing the right job in the right place and at the right time.

Weed Control

The harm that weeds do to fruit crops is obviously much less than that inflicted by pests and diseases. Nevertheless, there are several important reasons why they should be prevented from becoming too numerous.

The first is purely aesthetic. No one likes to see a garden, or even a section of one, choked with weeds. It looks awful and gives the impression of slovenliness.

The next point concerns the whole garden. If weeds are allowed to flourish and prosper in one part of it, they will quickly spread from end to end. The idea that weeds will stay in one place is ridiculous and it is usually the worst weeds that are the most invasive. Bindweed and ground elder are two examples; if these are left to themselves, they will quickly expand their territory.

The most damaging thing that weeds do is to compete with cultivated plants for the food and water that is present in the soil. Although the obvious sufferers are the smaller fruit plants, like strawberries and raspberries, those higher up the scale can also suffer.

Because weeds are largely spreading and shallow rooted, they are able to intercept much of the water that lands as rain. Although the same can hardly be said about plant nutrients, the weeds will certainly take their share of any fertilisers applied. This, in fact, is recognised by commercial fruit growers who will sometimes control the vigour of their trees and bushes by either allowing weeds to grow beneath them or by killing them.

The same effect is achieved by sowing grass below fruit trees to reduce their growth rate and induce fruitfulness. It just shows how great the effect of weeds can be even on something as large as trees and bushes.

Of course, in the case of strawberries, weeds not only represent competition, but,

Applying weedkiller amongst fruit trees with a dribble-bar attachment to eliminate drift; this is also particularly important for crops such as strawberries.

if allowed to grow unchecked, their size can actually smother and stunt the plants.

A particularly annoying and apparently immortal weed amongst bush and cane fruits is bindweed. This wraps itself around the shoots and branches, often right to the top. It can even delay ripening of the fruits by shading them from the sun, as well as making it far harder to pick them. Most weeds, though, are simply competing for water and nutrients.

As with pests and diseases, the best time to control weeds is before they do any harm. Usually, the simplest method of control is hoeing, but only when the ground is dry enough. You only have to touch the weeds when they are tiny to kill them. Later on, when they are a couple of inches or so high, they can still be hoed out, but this may not always be easy and, anyway, they will already be competing with the fruit by then.

The golden rule with annual weeds is to kill them before they are in flower. Once they reach this stage, they will usually set seed, even if they are subsequently killed. When hoeing weeds that are in flower, always rake them up afterwards and put them straight on the compost heap.

If weeds need to be killed but hoeing is impossible, a chemical weedkiller is usually the answer, although a good mulch of garden compost in the spring will often prevent them coming in the first place.

There are many weedkillers to choose from, but, for annual weeds and seedling perennials, a diquat-based one ('Weedol') is the quickest and easiest and it kills the weeds almost instantly. For established perennial weeds, like ground elder, thistles and bindweed, glyphosate is much more effective as it is systemic in action and, thus, gets right down into the roots. Several products are based on this. Both these materials are absorbed solely through the leaves and are inactivated by contact with the soil.

If there is grass growing intentionally beneath trees, any broad-leaved weeds can usually be killed with a lawn weedkiller.

A natural alternative to the hoe and the weedkiller is a good mulch, as already mentioned. This is a grand smotherer of weeds and is usually most effective when applied just after the seedlings have appeared. The mulch kills the tiny plants and prevents any more coming up.

Of course, a more attractive way of keeping weeds down is to grow ground-cover plants; but then you have to remember that they too will be competitors!

6 Pruning and Growth Control

PRUNING

To the beginner, pruning is always one of the more mystifying jobs in the garden. Where fruit trees are concerned there are strange words like 'laterals', 'spurs' and a host more to cope with. Do we really have to know what all these mean?

To be honest, no; but it does help to know a few basic expressions because they will keep cropping up when you read about the subject.

To begin with, though, it would be as well to look at the reasons for pruning fruit at all. There are two that overwhelm all others and neither could be said to be the more important because both have to be borne in mind.

They are, first, to shape the tree or bush and, second, to maintain a balance between growth and fruiting. One can add more factors to these, such as encouraging fruiting or encouraging growth, the removal of dead, broken and diseased shoots and branches and those that are in the wrong place. All these are part of pruning and have to be considered, but they are 'how' you prune, not 'why'.

A fruit tree or bush that isn't pruned will certainly not die, but it will go progressively downhill with age – along with the quality and quantity of fruit. It will stop growing and, as in the wild, it will become congested with shoots and branches which periodically die.

Having established the benefits of pruning, therefore, what are the tools that you will need?

First, a good pair of secateurs. These are of two basic designs: scissor or anvil action. The first explains itself while, in the anvil type, the blade presses onto an alloy or hard plastic pad. The scissor ones cost more, but give a cleaner cut.

The other tool that will be needed if you are dealing with large trees is a good pruning saw. Forget any nonsense about carpentry saws; these are useless for the job and will probably be ruined. The handiest type is a small, hollow-ground, folding saw. It takes up very little room and gives a beautiful smooth cut. Pruning saws cut when pulled, not when pushed.

A couple of other tools that might be handy are a pair of loppers and a long-arm pruner. The loppers are for cutting branches that are too thick for secateurs but awkward for reaching with a saw, such as in black currant bushes. The long-arm pruner is, obviously, for pruning parts of the tree that are out of reach from the ground.

All these tools will be useful all over the garden, not just with the fruit, so it pays to buy good ones. They must also be kept properly sharp at all times; blunt tools are useless and will damage the wood you are trying to cut.

Having looked at the reasons for pruning and the tools needed, what happens to a tree or bush when it is pruned? What are the effects of pruning?

There are two basic facts relating to pruning fruit trees and bushes. One is that cutting a shoot back encourages it to grow. The other is that an unpruned shoot will produce more fruit buds and produce them quicker than a pruned one. In practical terms, if a one-year-old shoot is shortened by half during the winter, two, three or even four new shoots will grow out from buds in the following year. If it had not been pruned, it would simply have got longer without producing any, or certainly fewer, side-shoots (laterals). In addition, many of the buds lower down would have developed into fruit buds.

With these two facts in mind, the gardener can decide which course he wants a particular shoot to take and act accordingly. That sounds terribly pat and easy and, in fact, pruning is quite easy when you understand what a particular action will result in. Of course, the skill comes when you find out that not all shoots act in the same way; it is as though some have never been told what the rules are.

Remember also that no cut should be made without a definite purpose.

PRUNING TREE FRUITS

Young Trees

By and large, the different kinds of tree fruit (apples, pears, etc.) are pruned in the same way to produce a particular tree form. That is to say, a bush tree is formed in much the same way whether it is an apple or a plum; it is only later that differences crop up.

A bush tree should have about 2ft (60cm) of clear trunk below the bottom branches. If you buy a ready-made bush tree,

and most people do, any branches more than an inch or two lower than that should be removed. Thereafter, pruning during the first few years must be to build up the main branches that will form the tree.

Each winter, the dominant shoot (leader) on each branch is cut back by about a third to induce laterals to develop. If a shoot is produced where it is not wanted, it can be left intact to fruit or, if it is in the way, shortened back or removed completely. Once the framework is formed, pruning will depend on the fruit concerned.

Half-standards are formed in just the same way except that the trunk should be 4ft (1.2m) tall.

If you are intending to grow spindle-bush apples and/or pears and are starting with a one-year-old 'whip' (single stem with no side-shoots), shorten it to 3ft (90cm) tall. If you are starting with a two- or three-year-old tree already having one-year-old side shoots, tip the side shoots and also the 'leader' (the main, central shoot).

To form a cordon tree, the central shoot is allowed to grow unhindered until it reaches the top training wire. When laterals develop directly from the main stem, prune them back to about 3in (7.5cm) long in late July to form fruiting 'spurs'.

If you start with a maiden tree, an espalier is formed by cutting it back to 2–3in (5–7.5cm) above the bottom training wire. The top bud will grow upwards to continue the main stem and the next two produce shoots which will be trained out sideways along the wire to form the first tier of horizontal branches; the initial cut should be made with this in mind. From then on, the system is roughly the same each winter, the top bud being for extension growth, the next two for a tier of branches.

Maiden peach and plum trees for fan-training should be cut back to 24in (60cm)

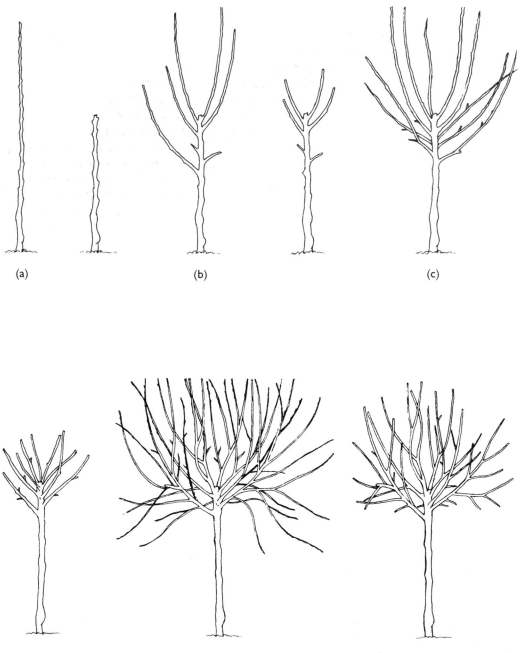

(a)

(b)

(c)

(d)

Bush and half-standard trees are formed in much the same way, the early years being concerned mainly with branch formation.

56

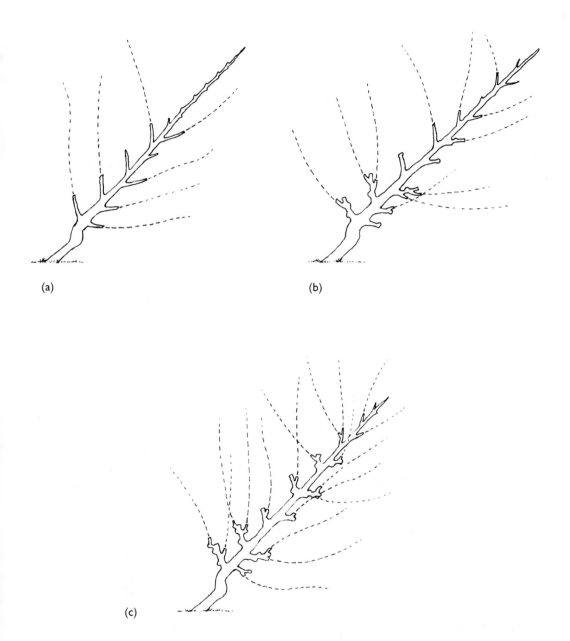

(a)

(b)

(c)

(a) to (c) Because cordons are grown as a single stem, all side shoots arising directly from that stem are shortened to 3in (7.5cm) long after planting and, subsequently, in the late summer. Those growing from previously shortened shoots are reduced to 1in (2.5cm).

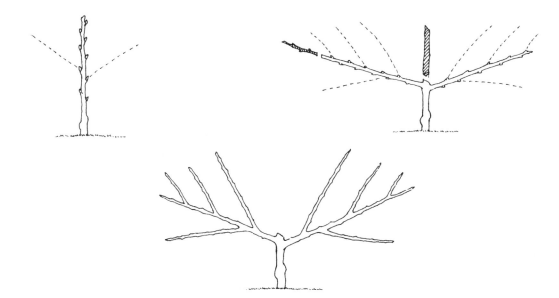

The first three years of a fan-trained tree's life.

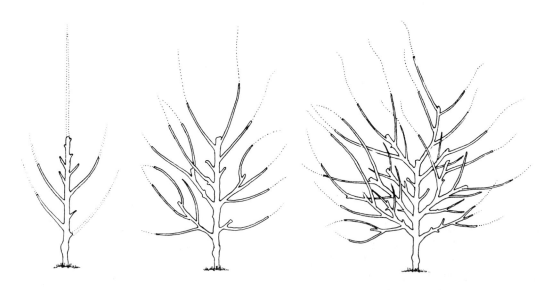

Dwarf pyramid. (Left) The newly-planted tree is cut back to 20in (50cm) tall. Any side shoots longer than 6in (15cm) are reduced to five buds. (Centre) Next winter, shorten the new leader growth to 8–10in (20–25cm) and new side shoots to 6–8in (15–20cm). (Right) In subsequent late summers, shorten the branch leader to 5–6in (12.5–15cm) long, the side shoots from branches to 3in (7.5cm) and those from existing side shoots to 1in (2.5cm).

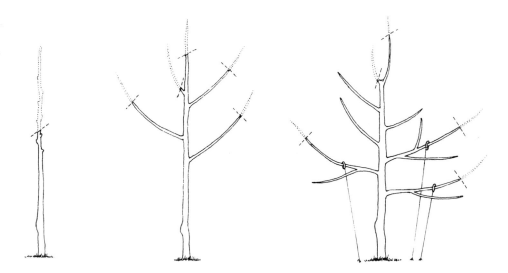

Spindlebush. (Left) If planting a maiden, cut it back to 3ft (90cm) after planting. (Centre) Next winter; shorten the side shoots and the central leader by about a third to induce further branching. The same treatment applies to a maiden tree already carrying side shoots (a feathered maiden). (Right) In the next summer (or one earlier, if dealing with a feathered maiden), well placed side shoots are tied down to 30 degrees above the horizontal. The one directly below the central leader is removed to prevent competition.

tall in the spring after planting. The aim is to produce two good laterals on opposite sides of the main stem no more than 1ft (30cm) from the ground. If there is already a suitable side-shoot 1–2ft (30–60cm) up the stem, keep it and shorten the main stem back to it.

If there are only buds (no side-shoots), wait until two well-placed shoots have started to grow out; the main stem above them can be cut back to the top one in the summer. In the following February, shorten back the two laterals to 12–18in (30–45cm) long and train them out at about forty-five degrees. Thereafter, cover the wall or fence by tying in suitable shoots and removing all others. On no account allow a central leader to form in a fan-trained tree. It will dominate it.

Established Trees

Apples and pears are pruned similarly, so can be dealt with together.

Standards, half-standards and bush trees are pruned in two basic ways: the regulated system and the renewal system.

The regulated system is the easier of the two and involves the removal of all branches that are dead, diseased, broken or in the way. The first three sorts are easy enough to spot, but branches that are 'in the way' needs explaining.

In the main, trees should have their centres cear of branches; this makes them easier to manage, less likely to attract pests and diseases and the fruit quality is improved. All branches that are crossing from one side of the tree to the other should, therefore, be removed. Similarly, all branches that are

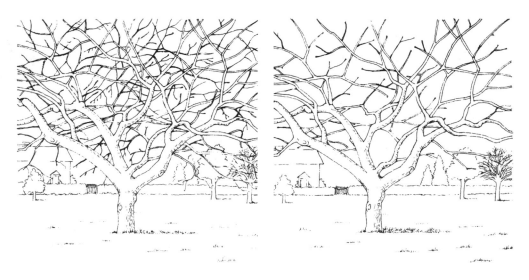

Regulated pruning, in which dead, diseased, broken, too high or too low branches and those causing overcrowding are removed.

either too high or too low should go. Others that must be pruned out, or back, are those which are clearly causing overcrowding.

With the renewal system, the same rules apply concerning the removal of un-wanted branches and shoots, but it is car-ried a stage further; This is why it leads to more and better fruit than the regulated system.

There is still the normal framework of branches, but, instead of these being the main cropping branches themselves, a suc-cession of smaller and renewable fruiting branches are carried on them. When these get either too high, too low or too old to fruit properly, they are replaced. The smaller branches that replace them are built up in the course of three to four years for that specific purpose. Thus, we have a tree that is furnished with main branches, fruiting branches and juvenile branches that are still developing.

When pruning standards, half-standard and bush plum trees, the regulated system

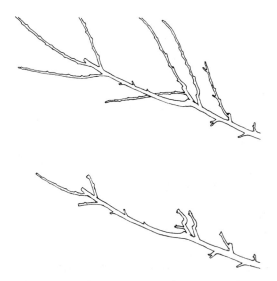

Spur pruning. The extension growth on the end of the branch is shortened by half and all side shoots arising directly from the branch are cut back to no more than 4in (10cm). Side shoots arising from existing spurs (already shortened side shoots) are cut back to 1in (2.5cm). This system of pruning is largely restricted to apple and pear cordons and espaliers.

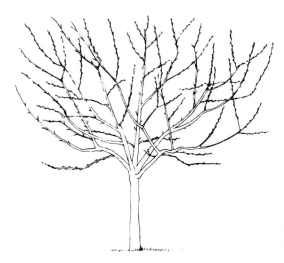

An apple tree pruned by the 'renewal' method, to encourage a constant supply of young and vigorous fruiting branches.

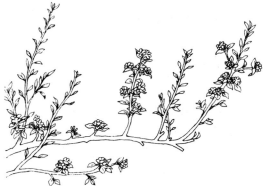

The main horizontal branch is well furnished with young growing and fruiting shoots. Once this branch bends down too far, it will be shortened back so that one of them takes its place.

is the one to bear in mind except that, on the whole, plums need considerably less attention. In fact, once they are cropping, the less they are pruned, the better.

Also, whereas apples and pears are pruned in the winter, plums should be left until there is a sign that the buds are moving in the spring – either that, or after fruiting. This is simply because plums are susceptible to the fungus disease Silver Leaf which is at its most dangerous in the winter. For the same reason, large saw cuts should always be painted over.

Cordon apples and pears are pruned solely in the summer once they have reached the top training wire. In early August, all new laterals that are hardening at their base (semi-ripe) and which are growing directly from the main stem are nipped back to 3–4in (75–10cm) long. Those growing from previously shortened side-shoots or spurs are taken back to 1in (2.5cm).

Any that are not semi-ripe are left and pruned a month later. Extension growths that come from the earlier pruning are cut hard back once the leaves have fallen. This does indicate, though, that the first pruning was done too early.

Espaliers are treated in just the same way as cordons, regardless of whether the shoots are arising from the horizontal arms of the tree or the upright central stem.

Once fan-trained plum trees have covered their allotted space, any shoots that are growing directly towards or away from the wall or fence are cut away as soon as they are seen in the growing season.

Those shoots that are required to extend a branch or fill a space are tied in as the summer progresses. Shoots not required for this should have their tops pinched out (stopped) when they reach 6–7in (15–17.5cm) long. These will form the fruiting spurs.

Peaches are treated somewhat differently because they only fruit on the shoots that grew in the previous year. In the spring, all badly placed shoots are cut away as for plums. Later, the remainder are tied to the training wires so that they are approximately 6in (15cm) apart along the top and bottom of the branch. Once these shoots have fruited in the following summer, they are either cut hard back to produce more shoots or they are tied in to fill any space.

PRUNING BUSH AND CANE FRUITS

Gooseberries, red currants and white currants are pruned in just the same way; so, what is recommended for gooseberries, applies equally well to all fruit best grown on spurs.

The bushes are grown on a short leg, or trunk, and any shoots that appear from below the bottom branches at any time should be removed.

After planting, young bushes should have all new shoots cut back by a third to a half to build up a good framework of semipermanent branches. When eight to twelve of these half-grown branches exist,

you can start pruning for fruit. This is done by shortening back all new side shoots to 1in (2.5cm) in the early winter. Thus, a fruitful spur system is created. The branch leaders are cut back by half so that extension growth can continue.

If time permits, summer pruning can take place in late June with the new shoots being stopped at about 4in (10cm) long. Winter pruning follows as usual.

Black currants fruit best on young wood so the bush consists of a stool with many of the shoots coming from below ground. After planting, all shoots should be cut down to within 2–3in (5–7.5cm) of the ground to promote vigorous and healthy growth in the following season. Little cutting back is required beyond shaping and keeping the bushes open and uncluttered.

With established bushes, once they reach four to five years old, any branches that have fruited for four seasons are best cut right out to encourage younger branches to replace them. If it seems that the bushes are getting crowded, whole

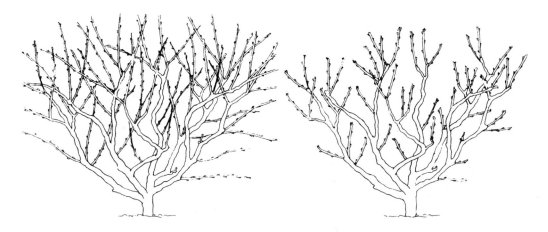

Gooseberry bushes before pruning (left) and afterwards. As with red currants, they are grown on a 'leg' and are made up of 8–12 main branches bearing fruiting spurs. The spurs are formed by shortening all side shoots to one bud in the early winter.

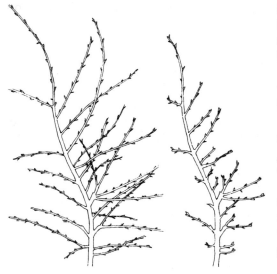

Close-up of gooseberry branch before pruning (left) and afterwards.

shoots or even branches should be cut out rather than snipping away genteelly with secateurs. This is where loppers come in handy!

When one comes to prune cane fruits, it is time that is required rather than knowledge.

Summer fruiting raspberries produce canes one year which fruit in the following July/August. Immediately after fruiting, these canes are cut down to the ground.

Autumn fruiting raspberries are entirely different in that the canes grow and fruit in a single year. The fruited canes are left until the following March when all are cut to the ground.

Blackberries, loganberries, tayberries etc. grow in exactly the same way as summer raspberries, so the fruited canes need to be cut right down after fruiting. Occasionally, a

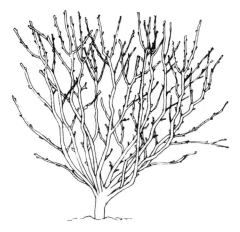
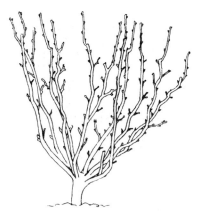

(Left) A red currant bush before pruning. (Right) After pruning. This consisted of cutting back all new side shoots on the main branches to about two buds.

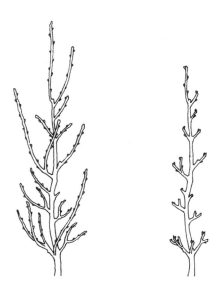

Close-up of red currant branch before pruning (left) and afterwards.

blackberry plant only produces one new cane from the stool during the summer. When this happens, it is permissible to shorten a fruited cane back to a strong new shoot near its base rather than remove it entirely.

RESTORATION WORK

One of the most disheartening things for any newcomer to gardening is to come face to face with an apparently centuries-old apple tree in their very first garden. It inspires a feeling of complete inadequacy and hopelessness.

However, as long as the problem is faced logically and in the proper sequence, there is no reason why the tree shouldn't

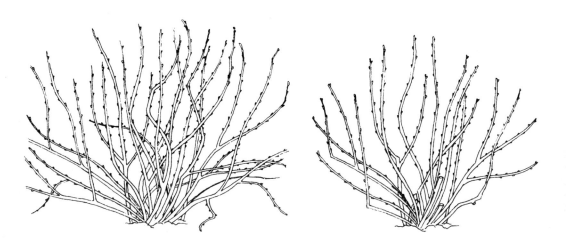

Black currant bush unpruned (left) and pruned. The bushes are grown as 'stools', with many shoots originating below ground. Sections of branch which are out of place are cut back as necessary, otherwise the only pruning is to remove completely any branch systems that fail to crop properly. This usually means any that are over about four years old.

'Merton Worcester' apple tree in bloom.

Fan-trained peach tree.

Espalier pear.

Spindlebush apple trees.

ABOVE: '*Elsanta*' *strawberries.*   *BELOW: A punnet of 'Cambridge Vigour' strawberries.*

'Elstar' apples.

'Grenadier' apples.

Comice pears.

'Concorde' pears.

'Garden Lady'
peach.

'Brown Turkey'
fig.

ABOVE: *'Cambridge' gage.*   BELOW: *'Marjorie's Seedling' – a cooking plum.*

'Lancashire Lad' gooseberries.

'Fantasia' blackberry.

be restored to full vigour. That is, provided that it is worth it.

Although large fruit trees are possibly the most awesome to tackle, the problem is not restricted to these and the first thing to decide is whether or not the 'subject' is really worth saving; bush and cane fruits seldom are. Very often, even a tree is just not worth the time and trouble. A new one can usually be bought inexpensively and will be cropping long before the old one has even recovered from the treatment. This has to be considered along with the question, 'do we want the thing anyway; good or bad? It may be taking up too much room or the variety could be poor.

Assuming, though, that you decide to keep a particular tree, the first task is to tackle it during the winter with a view to knocking it into shape. It is much easier to see what is happening if it is leafless. If the tree is old, the first thing to do is to get it growing again.

Renovation is not the sort of work to undertake with a pair of secateurs; it is something that has to be done in a business-like way with a proper pruning saw so that the problem is cured in one fell swoop. Never be frightened of taking out quite large branches; as long as they are the right ones, no harm will be done and the tree will be all the better for it.

First, then, get rid of any dead, diseased, dying or clearly out of place branches. This last category will include branches that are too high, too low or which spread out too far. What remains should be worth saving but, normally, there will still be far too many, so thinning out is called for. If it looks as though a lot of branches will have to go, it is often worth taking two winters over it. If it is all done at once, you can get such a lot of new growth that you are in just as bad a mess as before.

With the obvious branches removed, the next job is to thin out the remainder. This stage is usually better planned from the ground; it can be difficult to get an overall view when perched on top of a ladder. Better still, have one person on the ground directing operations and the other up the ladder carrying them out, normally with a saw.

The branches to remove first, if not already done so, should be any that are shooting up into the sky or trailing on the ground. There is very little point in keeping branches that are going to be a perpetual nuisance or which you will never be able to pick or prune. Then see if you can spot any key branches that are causing overcrowding; these must come out as well.

With younger trees that have simply become overgrown through recent lack of attention, the job will be a lot easier as the problem will be one of size rather than lack of fruit.

A good idea is to use a draw-hoe to scrape off much of the old and scaly bark that has built up on the trunk and main branches. You would be astonished at how many pests will be nicely tucked up for the winter under the bark scales.

You will probably have to spray several times during the following summer. You are unlikely to solve all the pest and disease problems in the first year, but persevere. The diseases scab and mildew are likely to be particularly bad on apple and pear trees, but you should never be surprised to see them return year after year; they do this even in the best commercial orchards.

Neglected trees are also going to need regular annual feeding. Although growth has to be encouraged, it should not be overdone, so a well balanced fertiliser, such as 'Grow-more', should be applied each February. This has equal parts (7 per cent) of nitrogen, phosphates and potash, so all the tree's natural functions are encouraged to get cracking again. Nitrogen is for growth and strong leaves and shoots. Phosphates encourage new roots to develop and potash leads to more and stronger fruit buds.

These jobs taken together, and given a couple of years or so, will restore the most uninspiring tree to fruitfulness and its former good looks.

VIGOUR CONTROL

Having just been told about putting the vigour back into fruit trees, it may seem a bit strange to be told now how to reduce it. However, this is not as contrary as it sounds. One of the causes of unfruitfulness in trees, especially, shall we say, teenage trees, is excessive vigour. If it is reduced, fruiting nearly always follows. There are a number of ways of doing so. Let us start with the easiest and gentlest, then work through to the hardest, most severe and least recommended and used – the horticultural 'if all else fails'.

The first remedy is to make sure that the union between the trunk and the rootstock is above ground. If it is buried, roots will grow from the trunk and the restricting effect of the rootstock will be reduced, or even completely overpowered. If you find that the union is covered, scrape away the soil and cut off any roots that are growing from the trunk. The soil should not be replaced or exactly the same thing will happen in a year or two.

If the union is not buried, try altering the fertiliser; assuming, that is, that you feed the tree. A common cause of excessive vigour is too much nitrogen. If, therefore, the nitrogen content of the fertiliser is higher than the potash level, change to one with more potash, such as a tomato

or rose food. In cases of extreme vigour, it may pay to give potash alone in the form of sulphate of potash. This method is effective, but it may take a year to show results.

In the section on weeds in Chapter 5, mention was made of using grass to control the vigour of trees. Grass seed is sown beneath over-vigorous trees in the spring. As the grass grows, it 'steals' some of the fertiliser and moisture from the ground that would otherwise have found its way down to the tree roots. This is a very quick way of altering the vigour of the tree and the opposite (getting rid of grass or weeds) is equally effective at increasing growth. The more ryegrass there is in the seed mixture, the greater the effect. Once the tree starts, or resumes, cropping, the grass can be cut hard or even killed or dug in.

These actions, either singly or in combination, will nearly always induce a tree to crop, but there are times when they will not. In this case, the remedy could be root pruning.

First, dig out a trench around the tree so that the inside is some 3ft (1m) out from the base of the trunk. The trench should be 2–3ft (60cm–1m) wide. While you are digging out the trench, save the small and fibrous roots and tie them back out of the way. These will be needed later to keep the tree alive; we want to reduce its vigour, not destroy it.

Any roots thicker than about 2in (5cm) across should have a section the width of the trench cut from them. This is needed to stop the two ends joining up again, as has been known to occur where only a single cut was made. It also gets them out of the way and makes any further digging easier. It will normally be sufficient to dig to 2ft (60cm) deep, but undercut any thick roots you find going straight down; these are often the very ones that are causing the excessive vigour.

Root pruning, to reduce a tree's vigour and encourage fruiting. A circle is first marked out 24–36in (60–90cm) away from the tree.

A trench is then dug outside the circle.

When the complete circle has been done, the retained roots are replaced and the trench filled in and firmed down.

As roots are exposed, sections of the larger ones are removed; the smaller roots are retained.

Once the operation is over, the trench should be refilled and the retained roots released and spread out carefully as the soil level rises. Firm them in well as you go.

The tree will need staking and should be watered during the following summer if there is the slightest indication that it is suffering.

Always root prune in the winter when the tree is dormant.

The final line of attack is 'bark ringing'. This should only be carried out if all else has failed. It involves removing a complete ring of bark from around the trunk of the tree so that the flow of sap is all but halted (hence its use as a last resort; it can be lethal if carried out carelessly).

The width of the ring (top to bottom) should never exceed ½in (1.25cm), even on the largest tree, and the wound must be bound with sticky tape immediately after removing the ring to prevent it drying out In the normal course of events, this has such a dramatic effect on the tree that fruit buds are often formed in profusion in the year after ringing for fruiting a year later. Don't let this encourage you to bark ring unnecessarily though; it's still a tricky business.

Bark ringing. This is only advised if all else fails to control an apple or pear tree's vigour. At blossom time, a complete ring of bark, no more than ½in (13mm) wide, is removed; the wound is taped in at once.

7   Picking and Storage

The picking and subsequent storage of fruit must surely be the most important part of the year. Having slaved for the previous twelve months to ensure that you have a worthwhile crop, here you are at last, at the moment of truth, when all your hopes are realised. That is, provided that you do the right thing at the right time.

Picking

How easy it would be in a surge of enthusiasm to ruin all the hard work by picking the fruit too early or, unlikely, too late.

Fortunately, strawberries, raspberries, blackberries and bush fruits (with the exception of gooseberries) give a clear indication of when they are ready for picking by changing colour to whatever they should be when mature.

With gooseberries, much depends on whether you want them for dessert or cooking. For cooking they are picked green at about the end of June. For dessert, they are left for another month or so until they go red or yellow, according to the variety. May Duke and Whinham's Industry are the leading red varieties; Laxton's Amber, Leveller and New Giant are yellow and most others are green.

A certain amount of confusion can exist amongst cane fruit because the hybrids tend to vary from dark pink to black when ripe. The tummelberry, for example, is raspberry coloured when ripe; loganberries and tayberries are somewhat darker; the boysenberry is very dark purple and the sunberry almost black. None should be picked until they have attained these colours because ripening after picking is seldom a success.

Although all kinds of fruit tend to ripen in sequence, true cooking gooseberries (for example Careless and Invicta) are normally cleared in a single picking. Much the same applies to red and black currants.

Early-ripening varieties of eating apple should be picked selectively so that they ripen on the tree. Those wanted for storing can be picked all at once later on.

Cooking apples are usually picked as they are needed, except those which you intend to store which are cleared at one picking. If any apples are still on the trees in the second half of October, they should be picked and stored.

Dessert pears are slightly harder to judge than apples, but are definitely better if picked when still hard and then ripened indoors. Cooking pears are picked and cooked when still hard.

Gages and dessert plums are normally picked over several times as they ripen; they don't ripen well after picking. When intended for cooking, though, plums are normally picked more severely as they are best when picked slightly under-ripe.

Peaches are best picked when ready for eating, but they will ripen quite well if immature ones are put on a sunny window sill.

Anyone extending into the realms of grapes and figs should leave figs until they are ripe, but grapes will ripen well after picking; though, frankly, there is little point in picking them early unless they are outdoors and spoiling.

The actual picking of most fruits is straightforward enough and most will part quite readily from the plant when they are fit.

When apples and pears are ready for picking, they part quite easily from the tree. In fact, the way to establish their readiness is to see how easy they are to pick. Lift the fruit and give it a slight twist. If it parts without any trouble, then that is as it should be. If you have to struggle with it, then wait a few days and try again. On the other hand, if it drops off the moment you touch it, then you have probably left it too long. Bear these points in mind when picking over the trees selectively. As already mentioned, apples and pears intended for storage are usually cleared at one picking.

Handling Fruit

When picking fruit, treat it all gently and carefully. Any damage that occurs will shorten the useful storage life.

If cane fruits, currants and strawberries are treated roughly, they will soon become infected with moulds and be useless.

Even more important is the way you handle apples and pears that are intended for storage. Any damage that occurs to them at any time before, during and after picking will ruin them for storage. This damage can be caused by a number of things. Pests, diseases, birds, wasps, rubbing and bruising are just some of the more obvious ones pre-harvest.

However, probably the greatest problems arise during picking itself when bruising and skin injuries are commonplace if picking is carried out carelessly. Every care

Lift the fruit and turn it half a circle. If it doesn't come away, it isn't ready for picking.

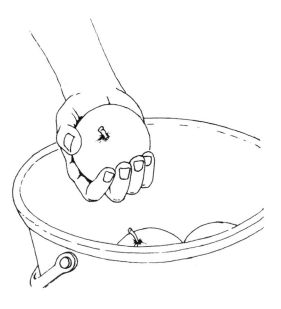

Place the fruit gently in a bucket or other container. Any damage to the skin will allow fungus diseases to infect it.

must be taken not to damage the fruits in any way. Treat them like eggs. Do not drop them into a bucket from the top of a ladder to save time; it saves nothing. Nowadays there are several picking aids that can be bought, but, to be quite honest, most are rather expensive for what they do and can usually be made at home without too much difficulty.

The main slant seems to be towards gadgets on the end of poles that can be raised up into tall trees to pick single fruits. These are mainly applicable to apples and pears, but there should be no reason why they cannot be used for plums as well. It is probably asking a bit too much to expect them to cope with cherries.

Another product works on the same principle but has a tubular canvas, or similar, chute attached so that the picked fruit rolls down the tube to the picker. This has the advantage of the picker not having to lower the gadget after picking three or four apples to empty the small canvas bag on the end of the pole.

When simply using a bucket or basket to pick fruit into, a bucket is much better as the inside of most shopping baskets are very knobbly and are much more likely to damage the fruit than the smooth surface of the bucket. In either event, it helps to line the container with a plastic bag so that, when full, this is lifted out and gently emptied by placing it in the box or whatever, simply removing the bag by pulling it out from under the fruits.

If you have a lot of tree fruits to pick, it would be well worthwhile investing in a proper fruit-picking bag. This is slung over the shoulder on a canvas strap and can then be swung round behind you when you are climbing up and down ladders. When picking from the ground, the bag would be in front of you.

These proper picking bags have a rigid top that stays open and a canvas body. This is open at the base which is folded up and held in place by two hooks on the upper rigid rim when you are picking. To empty it, stand the basket in the box and slip the two hooks off the rim so that the fruit gently flows out through the bottom when the bag is lifted. If done slowly, damage to the fruit is completely avoided.

Storage

The suitability of the various fruits for some form of storage has changed dramatically in the last twenty years with the arrival of freezers. Hitherto, only apples and pears could be kept whole for any length of time; other fruits had to be bottled or canned.

Now, most fruits can be frozen; either in their natural form, stewed or puréed. The only real problem remaining is that, notably, raspberries and strawberries collapse on thawing. This, though, always seems a small price to pay for the luxury of having them at any time of the year. As regards strawberries, there are now varieties becoming available that have a far better internal colour and which don't collapse like a jelly on thawing. Totem is one of these.

The only fruits that can be stored for any length of time *au* naturel are still certain varieties of apples and pears.

As a rule, apple varieties which ripen during November and later should be picked before maturing and then stored until ripe. If they are left on the trees, they run the risk of being ruined by either birds, weather or both.

The time at which apples and pears should be picked for storage is a little more precise than just guessing that they look about ready. In fact, it is one of the hardest tasks you are likely to be faced with when

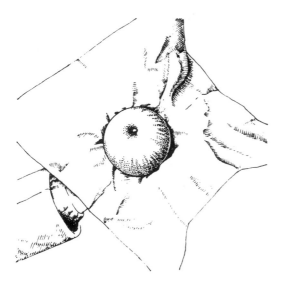

When storing late-ripening varieties, ideally wrap them individually in special paper and lay them gently in a wooden or cardboard box. Don't wrap them in newspaper; it is very absorbent and will draw moisture from the fruit. If you can't get the special paper, lay them unwrapped.

growing fruit because there are no hard and fast rules; too many variable factors come into it – for example variety, rainfall, temperature and the amount of sunshine.

All these factors will have an effect on the picking time and also the potential storage life of the fruit. Ripening is a very complex process, but we know quite a lot about it now, which helps. From the practical angle, early varieties like Discovery and Worcester Pearmain are best left on the trees to ripen and develop their flavour. Mid-season varieties, such as Cox, can either be left on the tree to mature or they may be picked in late September and stored. The choice really depends on when you want to eat them.

In some districts, birds will start to feed on the fruit long before it's ripe. Then there is always the risk that the whole lot will be brought crashing to the ground by autumn gales. Yet another problem, especially in the north, is the risk of severe frosts early in the winter.

Late-maturing varieties, those ripening after Christmas, certainly need to be picked and stored in all but the most sheltered and protected gardens.

In spite of the difficulties and variables, the point at which to pick apples and pears for storing is, technically, when internal activity is at a minimum. This occurs when the fruit has reached maximum size. Very soon after that, ripening starts, so the aim is to pick the fruit intended for storage during this lull. At that point, cool temperatures will postpone the onset of ripening, but delaying picking until after that will simply slow down ripening. Storage at just below 40°F will usually give the longest home-storage life.

But how, without a laboratory, does one judge the moment to pick? The short answer is simply by spending a lifetime at it.

Pears usually hang on a bit harder than apples, but they should never need to be tugged at and, if they seem to bring bits of tree off with them, then clearly you are being too heavy handed and too early.

While the best time to pick a variety for storing is when it has reached its maximum size but before it has started to mature (shown by a slight change in the ground colour), the date at which it will be ready to eat is a little more elastic. This will depend on the variety and the storage conditions.

Here are some examples of average picking dates and maximum storage dates for varieties of apple.

Dessert
Blenheim Orange   Late Sept. until Nov.–Jan.
Cox   Last week Sept. until Nov.–Jan.

Egremont Russet   Late Sept. until Oct.–Nov.

Greensleeves (new)   Mid-Sept. until Oct.–Nov.

Jupiter (new)   Mid-Sept. until Oct.–Jan.

Laxton's Superb   Early Oct. until Nov.–Jan.

Lord Lambourne   Mid-Sept. until Sept.–Nov.

Spartan (new)   Early Oct. until Nov.–Feb.

Sturmer Pippin   Mid-Oct. until Jan.–April.

Cooking

Annie Elizabeth End Sept. until Nov.–April

Bramley Seedling Mid-Oct. until Dec.–March

Lane's Prince Albert Late Sept. until Dec.–March

Lord Derby Late Sept. until Oct.–Dec.

Newton Wonder Mid–Oct. until Nov.–March

When planning to store apples, the first job is to find somewhere answering as many of the requirements of good storage conditions as possible.

Temperature is the first requirement. This should be constant and, ideally, above but close to freezing. However, it is unlikely that you will find anywhere much below about 10°C (50°F) in October capable of storing boxes of apples.

Avoid a stuffy and still atmosphere, this encourages disease in the fruit. The air should also be moist so that the fruit stays firm.

The store should be in darkness. In the light, chemical changes take place within the fruit which shorten its storage life.

The place most likely to answer all these requirements is a cellar. Failing that, a good stout outbuilding or garage will do, preferably brick or stone and with a solid floor Try to avoid small wooden sheds; the temperature within changes greatly and frequently.

Always remove tins of paint and other strong-smelling things from the vicinity of the apples for fear of taint; onions are especially likely to do this.

The best way to store apples is to wrap each fruit individually in paper and then pack them in boxes. They last well like this and any rots are prevented from spreading to touching fruits by the paper.

Storing apples in polythene bags is quite a good system, provided that not too many are involved. The fruits do not need to be wrapped. Never seal the bag completely, however; this causes a build-up of carbon dioxide. Simply fold the top under when it is full.

You can always keep just a few apples in the bottom of the fridge.

Most of what has been said about apples applies equally well to pears, but there is one big difference: the method of storage.

Pears keep much better and can be inspected easier if they are laid out on shelves or racks in the storage place; they are seldom happy wrapped and packed away in boxes.

When apples and pears are brought out of store and into the house, remember that it could be ten to fourteen days before they are ready for eating. Pears, in particular; are all too often as tasteless and hard as turnips and need this time to mature.

Exhibiting

An aspect of picking that sometimes crops up is picking for exhibiting in the local flower show. Apart from the obvious point of the fruits having their characteristic colour, an important point is that the stalks should always be left in place; even on strawberries and cane fruits.

Also, no fruit must on any account be polished, especially apples. Any natural bloom on the skin should be left as intact as possible. Grapes and plums have a particularly heavy bloom which should be kept.

Another useful tip concerns the varieties that you may want to show. Always exhibit fruits that are ready for use; immature and overripe specimens are not good enough. Further than this, you should only show apples, pears and plums that are in season at the time of the show. So often one sees Cox exhibited in September shows when they have no business to be there until October at the earliest. Although they are undeniably ready for picking in late September, they are nowhere near ready for eating.

The more exotic kinds of fruit that you may be growing for the first time will sometimes present a maturity problem to the gardener. In most cases, it is just a question of looking at the fruit and seeing how they feel. If they feel soft and look as though they should be ready for picking, then they probably are.

Melons, for example, should be pressed gently at the end where the flower was. If the flesh gives a little, you should then turn your attention to the stalk end. If you see a line developing around the point where the stalk joins the fruit, then you can be pretty sure that the fruit is ripe. If, when twisted slightly to one side, the fruit parts, you know it is fit to eat.

Many people say that you should go by the smell of the melon to see whether it is ripe or not, but even unripe specimens will have the characteristic smell, so that is not a reliable method. Stick to testing the soft flower end and the condition of the stalk.

8 Fruit in the Greenhouse

Before going too deeply into the practical aspects of actually growing fruit in greenhouses, it would be as well to start the story at the beginning by looking at the greenhouse itself and the various pieces of equipment that may, or may not, be needed.

We have to assume for a start that the greenhouse is not going to be used solely for the production of fruit. In most households this would be wholly uneconomical and would rather restrict one to growing exotics like pineapples and bananas, both of which, incidentally, are perfectly possible in this country. The sort of greenhouse we are talking about here is the ordinary run-of-the-mill type that any gardener would be only too happy to own.

If it is heated, so much the better because this will enable you actually to force fruits, and other plants, into maturity earlier than in an unheated house. However, heating is by no means an essential part of growing fruit; unless, as already mentioned, you are proposing to go in for exotics. But with heat, there comes the ability to raise your own bedding and half-hardy plants so, although not vital, it's a big advantage.

Even before that, though, you should sit down and work out just where the greenhouse is going to be sited. Obviously much will depend on the size and shape of the garden, but a number of considerations should be taken into account.

Siting the Greenhouse

It should be in a sunny position and not overhung by trees. Apart from the shade they may cast, there is always the risk of any falling branches landing on the greenhouse.

A windy site should be avoided. Not only does the wind have a terrific cooling effect, but there is also the chance that the greenhouse could be damaged by moving during gales.

If you want to have mains electricity or water in the greenhouse, make sure that it is sited near a source of either or both of these; it will reduce the cost of installing them.

Try not to site it in too prominent a position so that it dominates the garden; greenhouses are seldom decorative enough for this. By the same token, be sure that a particular position does not create awkward little nooks and crannies that you cannot reach with a mower or where you otherwise make work for yourself.

It's a good idea to keep greenhouses well away from children's play areas; greenhouses and children are notoriously incompatible, especially where ball games are concerned.

It sounds obvious, but never build a greenhouse on a slope. Nothing ever opens or closes easily and you will always have trouble with the staging being at an angle.

Type of Greenhouse

Having sorted out a suitable site, or given up the whole idea, you will need to consider whether this will call for a free-standing model or a lean-to. Both have their virtues and vices.

Although a free-standing house gives you more room for growing plants, a lean-to, especially if against the house, is usually easier to plumb in or wire from an adjoining room. It will also stay warmer longer, making use of the heat that the house wall absorbs during the day and releases at night. Also, it will be closer at hand, with the result that you will probably pay more attention to it.

The main problem with a lean-to is that you have little choice in where to position it; sunny walls can be few and far between. Added to that, lean-tos tend to be darker than free-standing models because all the light comes from one direction.

Deciding on the size and shape of the greenhouse can also be tricky, but you should always try to buy the largest that you can afford, bearing in mind that large greenhouses cost more to heat than small ones. This seems an obvious point, but is one that is often forgotten. Most gardeners tend to grow more plants than they can possibly house, so a big greenhouse is clearly of benefit.

The shape of the greenhouse is usually of much less importance, but it is always better to stick to a traditional rectangular one. Most of the different accoutrements that are available for equipping a greenhouse are geared to rectangular models. It's also more expensive to obtain unusually shaped bits of glass when breakage occurs.

Probably the most frequently asked question when it comes to choosing a greenhouse is whether it should be wood or metal. Once again, both have their virtues and vices.

Wood is a comparatively soft material which will easily take screws, nails and anything else that you may want to stick into it; metal is not and will not. Wood is also a warmer material than aluminium, so that wooden greenhouses tend to be warmer in the winter than metal ones, other things being equal. Whether stained or painted, a wooden house always looks more natural and more at home in a garden than a metal one. This may seem a small point, but a garden should be nice to be in and to look at.

The greater weight of a wooden greenhouse makes it more stable in gales.

Clearly, there are problems with a structure made of wood and the biggest is that, every couple of years or so, the wood needs treating with paint or preservative. Even if a metal greenhouse isn't looked after, it will last longer than a wooden one.

Metal greenhouses have narrower glazing bars and, therefore, admit more light. This isn't especially important for fruit, but seedlings during the spring can do with all the light they can get.

Aluminium has been mentioned as a suitable metal for greenhouses and, indeed, this is really the only metal worth considering. Steel is heavy to handle, which makes it difficult to get home and harder still to erect. Added to that, with its increased strength, putting in any fixtures and fittings can be a major operation.

As for glazing materials, glass is really the answer. The only places where it might be sensible to go for thick plastic of the Perspex type is where breakages are likely to occur frequently or where, for some reason, its lighter weight is an advantage. Glass is also a lot cheaper.

Nowadays, it might be well worth considering a polythene-glazed house, particularly if fruit is going to be the main occupant. Polythene certainly does not retain as much heat as glass, but this could be an advantage with hardy fruits because the greenhouse won't overheat so easily. Also, polythene has to be replaced every three years or so, though this is a small price to pay compared to the far smaller initial outlay.

Bearing in mind that most of the fruits you are likely to be growing in the greenhouse are hardy or half-hardy, a more important aspect than heating the structure is keeping it cool. This can be a real problem in a good summer.

It is essential to have efficient and effective ventilators. They should also be present both in the ridge and sides of the greenhouse. Fortunately, this is becoming standard practice with manufacturers and it is certainly a feature that should be insisted upon. Ridge vents will let out the hot air all right, but you need side vents to ensure a free circulation of cooling, fresh air amongst the plants. It is well worth considering louvre vents for the side of the greenhouse as, unlike conventional ventilators, they will not get in the way when opened.

Guttering is hardly something that would spring to mind when buying a greenhouse, but one that has gutters is preferable to one without. To start with, they carry water away from the body of the greenhouse which would otherwise simply splash onto the ground and cause problems. In addition, the water can be collected and fed into a water butt for use in the greenhouse. Rainwater is always better to use than tapwater, particularly in hard water areas.

EQUIPPING YOUR GREENHOUSE

Buying the greenhouse and putting it up is not, unfortunately, the only expense with which you will be faced. You can certainly start the ball rolling without any added equipment and gadgets but you will soon want to expand your interests.

For instance, you may well find that staging is not included in the basic price.

Staging

This is where you might start reaping the benefit if you have bought a wooden greenhouse because it really is quite easy to make and install your own staging if you wish to.

For most purposes, it is a good idea to have staging on just one side of the house; preferably the south or west. This is so that the smaller plants on the staging will not then have shadows cast on them by the taller ones standing on the ground along the other side.

On the staging will obviously go all the seedlings etc. that you will be raising in the normal course of gardening. However, it can also be used for strawberries in pots or other containers that are in the greenhouse during the early part of the year for forcing.

The ground on the opposite side of the house will be used for standing pot grown trees on. In some cases where a larger than usual greenhouse is being used, this border on the other side of the greenhouse may be planted with peaches, nectarines or apricots, or possibly a grapevine. Normally, however; the tree fruits mentioned are fantrained against the back wall of a lean-to house where they take up very little room but revel in the sunshine and warmth.

Depending on the kinds of fruit you are growing, or intend to grow, you may find that temporary staging is more convenient than a fixed set-up. If this is the case, one of the most convenient materials is corrugated asbestos, or its modern equivalent. This can be placed on legs to raise it to the desired height and then covered with gravel or lightweight aggregate for a level surface. If the sheet is large, drill some drainage holes in the troughs.

You may also find it handy to have shelves as well as staging in the greenhouse and, here again, this is often where a wooden house scores over a metal one.

Shelves can go on either or both sides of the house, depending on how much you need, but never make them too wide or they will need special strengthening to make them safe and sound; 6–8in (15–20cm) is about right. They can be usefully employed for holding seedtrays and pots up to about the 5in (13cm) size. The whole object of the exercise is to make the most economical use of the greenhouse and its heat but, at the same time, to grow what you most want; in this case, a fair amount of fruit.

Floor Covering

Some thought will also have to be given to the floor covering, both under the staging and over the rest. The normal routine is to leave it as bare earth under the staging; this allows drainage water from above to soak away and you'd be surprised at just how many shade-loving plants you can grow in pots under there.

A path should be made down the middle of the house and, here, you can use a number of materials. Remembering that this area is going to take a lot of use, it should be covered with something durable like paving stones, concrete or bricks. It is really a question of which is going to be the cheapest and easiest to come by.

If a large number of trees in pots or other containers are envisaged, it might pay to continue the hard-standing right up to the other side but, usually, the pots are stood either on the bare earth or on slates or tiles.

However, something is required under the pots or you will very soon find that worms work their way into the compost and create serious difficulties with the watering and the structure of the compost in the pots. As a temporary measure for use at certain times of the year, slatted duck-boarding can be put down for the pots to stand on.

Insulation

From the fruit's angle, insulation from the cold will not be needed; most of the plants that we will be growing in the greenhouse are perfectly hardy. However, if you want to keep a reasonable winter temperature in the house during the winter for other occupants, bubble plastic is a godsend. For the fuel that it saves, it costs very little and has the advantages over a single sheet of polythene of giving better insulation against the cold and also of being much less likely to encourage the formation of condensation. That has always been the curse of single-thickness polythene sheeting.

Shading

The opposite requirement to insulation is shading and this is going to be needed in the summer to stop the temperature rising dangerously high.

Whitewash has long been the traditional material for shading. Painted on the outside of the glass, it keeps a lot of the sun's rays out without creating gloomy conditions inside. There are more sophisticated equivalents now though, possibly the best being one that almost disappears when the sun is in, but which intensifies when the light strengthens.

Although these are perfectly satisfactory, the netting kind of shading is better, provided that you rig up a system for raising and lowering it as the conditions dictate.

The Rolls Royce treatment, though, is a set of roller blinds that are pulled up and let down as required. Needless to say, this is also the most expensive system.

On the same subject of keeping the plants cool, it is well worth fitting an automatic opener to at least one of the roof vents. This ensures that some cool air is getting into the house even when there is no one there to look after it.

Heating

As heating is not the main requisite of fruit under glass, it will be sufficient to say here that the most you will normally be called upon to provide is sufficient to keep the frost out once growth has started in the spring. Always remember, however, that spring starts a good deal earlier under glass than in the open. With this in mind, a paraffin heater is usually ample. However, it must be a good one so that fumes and smoke are not given off; these will seriously damage young growth and blossom, as and when they appear. The blue-burner type is normally the most satisfactory. A step up in efficiency, and less likely to give any problems, is the propane-burning type.

Watering

As far as watering the plants is concerned, it must always be remembered that you can never rely on enough water falling as rain. This is an obvious comment for plants in the greenhouse, but it applies equally well to those in pots which are standing out in the open.

There are several aids to watering, such as drip-irrigation kits and capillary matting, but most gardeners will rely on their own judgement.

Grapes and peaches planted in the border soil will normally have enough water at the roots once they have been established for a few years; they are roughly the same as trees planted in the open. However, during periods of water stress in the summer, it could well be necessary to provide them with extra. This is particularly important when the fruit is setting and then swelling.

Most trees growing in pots will be outside during the summer and will need attention every day; if they run short of water during the growing season and when they are carrying fruit, they can well suffer.

How often they will need watering is anyone's guess; it depends on the weather, the amount of root in the pots, the size of the plants and how much the natural rainfall supplies. To give a rough guide, though, they should be looked at every day during the growing season in case they need watering. When the surface of the compost dries out, it will be safe to water because, provided that the drainage is as good as it should be, any surplus will run through. Having already moved slightly into the cultivation side of greenhouse fruit growing, it would be as well not to proceed further without looking at the subject in a much more general way so that, in effect, we start at the beginning.

The idea of growing fruit in a greenhouse probably conjures up a picture of Georgian orangeries. Not a bit of it; you can perfectly well use the old 8 × 6ft greenhouse that you've been keeping rabbits in. The only difference is the scale of the operation.

CHOICE OF FRUITS

Once the greenhouse is in place and all the necessary equipment is installed, and this doesn't really amount to any more than you would need for a greenhouse anyway, there comes the choice of fruits to grow.

To begin with, it is possible for you to grow kinds of fruit that wouldn't stand a chance outside in Britain. Bananas and pineapples have already been mentioned, but, to these, we can add the many different kinds of citrus fruits (oranges, lemons etc.).

Then there are the fruits that are borderline for growing outdoors successfully. They survive outside and, in a good summer, they crop reasonably well, but they operate far better with the protection of a greenhouse for all or just part of the year. These include fruits such as peaches, nectarines and apricots, figs, grapes and melons. We should really add Kiwi fruit (Chinese gooseberries) to these because, quite honestly, they are far from a success outdoors in the mainland UK. In fact, the only people growing them commercially are owners of large heated greenhouses in the Channel Isles; many of them gave up tomatoes to do so.

Leaving aside the kiwis, which would be planted in the greenhouse soil, the others can be planted either in the greenhouse borders or in pots so that they can be moved in under cover at critical times of the year but otherwise stay outside. This system will stretch the list to include our own perfectly hardy apples, pears, plums and cherries.

Lastly, the greenhouse can be used to produce fruit out of season, and this can mean either early or late. Strawberries are an example of this kind.

Citrus Trees

Unfortunately, genuine exotics need rather special conditions to be successful and these can be very costly for the ordinary gardener to achieve, especially when it comes to the heating. However, provided that the frost can be kept out and that just a little extra warmth is available, citrus fruits are perfectly simple to grow. In fact, there's no reason why they shouldn't be grown from pips, but you do run the same risk as with apples and pears; namely, that it's unlikely that the progeny will be anything like the parent. For this reason, it's always better to buy young plants from a specialist nursery rather than to take a chance.

If you propose to grow trees in the greenhouse border, you must first make sure that the soil is well drained and slightly on the acid side. Very few fruits are a success in alkaline soil.

For pot cultivation, John Innes Potting compost No. 3 is a good choice. A soil-based compost like this is preferable to a peat compost because it adds far greater stability to the plant and the loam content acts as something of a buffer against sudden changes in temperature and water content. Clay pots also add weight, but they are by no means essential if a soil-based compost is being used.

If only a minimal amount of heat is available, oranges will still be quite all right, but the temperature must not be allowed to drop to freezing and the plants will need to be kept only just on the moist side of bone dry in the winter. Growth will start in March/April and the plants usually flower in the summer. This leads to the fruitlets overwintering in a small and green state, after which they will grow on and mature in the summer.

For those gardeners with a little more heat at their fingertips, a minimum of 45–50°F (7–10°C) will bring them into flower in February, which will give rise to ripe fruit in the period October–January.

With both these systems, there is no reason why, if the trees are growing in pots, they should not be put outside in a sunny and sheltered position from June–August.

Grapevines and Peach Trees

It has been the practice for countless years to use the greenhouse to produce better and larger crops from kinds of fruit which are normally quite happy growing outdoors. There used to be scarcely a large house anywhere that didn't boast a peach tree and a grapevine growing under glass. More often than not, a whole greenhouse would be given over to their cultivation. These were normally lean-to houses in the walled garden with grapes occupying the lower portion of roof and peaches, nectarines and apricots fan-trained to the wall behind. This can still be seen in some of our larger and older country houses, but the sight is becoming rarer every year. Most have been replaced with crops like tomatoes which can be sold to defray some of the ever-mounting costs.

Grapes and peaches are still popular, though, and there is no reason why they should not be grown in all but the smallest greenhouse. To give you an idea, you will need an area of at least 6ft square (4sq.m) to house a fan-trained peach tree.

Today, grapes are usually planted outside the greenhouse and then led through a hole in the wall before being trained to the roof. This isn't the best method as, in the spring, the top growth starts growing before the roots, but it does leave the greenhouse border free for other crops, such as tomatoes. It is so much easier to use growing-bags for the tomatoes though, and it means the vine can be planted indoors.

A young vine being planted in the greenhouse border. Don't allow the roots to dry out when doing this and spread them well out.

Grapes are not too fussy as to soil type, but it must be free draining and contain plenty of organic matter. A good way of doing this is to prepare a planting position 3ft square (1sq.m) and 3ft (1m) deep. Early spring is the best time for planting, but autumn and mild spells during the winter are quite acceptable.

Always try to buy a two-year-old plant that is growing in a pot. This is planted with the roots teased out of the rootball and only the strongest shoot retained, if there is more than one. This is cut back to a bud about 1ft (30cm) from the ground or, if planted outside and brought in, to the first two buds inside the greenhouse.

Black Hamburgh is probably the best black grape for growing under glass in Britain and it has excellent quality.

We cannot adopt quite the same routine with peaches, which must be planted in the greenhouse and then trained up a wall. This makes a lean-to house more or less essential. With an ordinary shaped house, it is better to grow the vine in a pot and treat it as described in Chapter 8. Although there are other good varieties, Peregrine peach and Lord Napier nectarine are hard to beat for all-round performance.

Peaches and nectarines need much the same soil conditions as grapes, but the border should be about 6ft (2m) long by 3ft (1m) wide with adequate drainage. The trees should be planted 5–6in (13–15cm) from the wall and leaning slightly towards it to make tying in easier.

Train the tree as a fan; this means that you will need horizontal training wires 6in (15cm) or two courses of bricks apart on the wall.

A fan-trained tree must never be neglected, which means that quite a lot of work will be needed during the summer, such as nipping out unwanted shoots, pinching back and tying in retained ones and two sessions of thinning the fruitlets. If you think that this is going to be too much to cope with, the answer could be to grow the tree in a pot instead.

(Left) A fan-trained peach tree in a greenhouse in winter. This is also the best tree form for outdoors.
(Right) Young peach trees in a greenhouse carry a useful crop.

GROWING IN POTS

Pots are a very good way of growing many kinds of tree fruit where space in the garden is limited but, of course, they have other advantages as well. Apples, pears, plums, cherries, peaches, nectarines, apricots and even grapes and figs can all be grown successfully in pots.

We have already seen a few of the benefits, but it would be as well to look at them now as a whole rather than piecemeal. The obvious one is that growing fruit in this way takes up virtually no room at all. This has clear benefits in small gardens, but it is also useful in larger ones because it allows you to grow a lot more kinds and varieties of fruit. You can even look upon it as a trial ground for something that you fancy, but would like to know more about before committing yourself to larger quantities.

The mobility of the trees is an enormous advantage; it allows them to be moved to different places. If this sounds rather pointless, don't forget that it is really the whole object of the exercise: the ability to move the trees under cover at times of the year when the weather is likely to damage them. The important time is in the spring when the trees can be brought into the greenhouse if a night frost threatens to destroy the blossom and new growth. Another time that protection is usually needed is in the autumn when gales are liable to bring off the ripening fruits.

By the same token, if you have a fruit cage, the pots can be moved in there when the fruit is ripening to protect them from birds and children.

On top of all this, there is what might be called the 'show-off' factor. If a tree in blossom or carrying fruit is placed in a suitably ostentatious position, it will undoubtedly cause raised eyebrows and will be the talking point of the neighbourhood.

Management

Despite all the advantages of this form of fruit culture, there are obviously problems, the main one being that trees in pots require quite a bit of attention during the summer. In addition, the smaller trees are clearly going to produce smaller crops than trees in the open ground. A problem that arises here is that, to produce a small tree in a pot, logic says that it should be on a dwarfing rootstock. Wrong. If a fruit tree on a dwarfing rootstock is planted in a pot, it will be dead in a few years. Why? Because a fruit tree on a dwarfing rootstock needs very good growing conditions to survive and thrive. In a pot, the growing conditions are far from good. In other words, a fruit tree in a pot is kept dwarf by the restrictions of the pot, not by the rootstock. So, under the restricted conditions already imposed by the pot, the tree needs a strong rootstock to survive.

Although it is of lesser importance, it is also wise to consider the choice of varieties in connection with their own vigour as well. Some are naturally stronger growing and may need a more dwarfing rootstock than others.

Because a much smaller tree is going to be grown, we must choose a suitable shape for it and it is generally accepted that the dwarf pyramid shape serves the purpose well. The main exceptions to this are peaches and nectarines which do better as open-centre bush trees. Figs are also different and should be fan-trained to a cane frame.

If you can, start with a two or three-year-old tree that has already been pruned to the basic shape; this means that it will at least start life by pointing in the right direction.

The pot, or other container, in which you are going to grow the trees should certainly not be too large. Don't be misled into thinking that, because you are dealing with a tree, the container has to be the size of a water butt. The pot size to start with is usually a 10in (25cm) one. It can progress over the years to a 12in (30cm) and 14in (35cm), but never start too large or the tree will put on too much growth and will not fruit for some time. All containers must have drainage holes.

We have already looked at the choice between clay and plastic containers and have come down on the side of clay for the sake of its stability; it also looks more the part. However, if you feel like breaking away from a true pot and going in for a more decorative container, modern moulded plastic troughs etc. are excellent, provided that you choose a good, thick one. Again, don't forget the drainage holes.

We have also touched on suitable composts and have come out in favour of John Innes Potting No. 3, but do make sure that it is a good make and that it comes from a reputable source; there are still some cheap brands about which are no good.

Potting Up

Now all is ready for potting up the trees. The container-grown trees available from garden centres today make life a lot easier as they already have a restricted root system so, in this respect, they are better than bare-rooted ones. Added to that, they can be potted up at any time of the year and not just in the winter, as with bare-rooted specimens.

When potting, the first thing to do is to put crocks over the drainage holes. This is followed by a ½ in–1 in (1.25–2.5cm) of coarse peat siftings, on top of which goes the first layer of potting compost. Containerised trees can then be put straight into the pot, after removing the container; and compost firmed down the sides. Plant it so that the tree is about an inch deeper than it was

previously. Leave about an inch of exposed rim at the top for watering. Give the whole thing a good soaking and the job is done.

Planting bare-rooted trees is carried out in just the same way except that, after the first few handfuls of compost have been returned, fidget the tree about so that the compost falls down between all the roots. Firm the compost down as you go. As a rule, repotting or potting on will only be needed every other year.

Feeding

Feeding is easy enough, but it does need regular attention during the growing season. With newly potted trees, the fertiliser in the compost will last about a month, but, soon after fruit-set in the spring, a dressing of a balanced feed, like 'Growmore', should be given. If the leaves turn pale in the summer, it means that the tree is hungry, but, instead of piling on more 'Growmore', change to fortnightly liquid feeding. This is quicker acting and you have more control over growth. Nowdays you can buy pellets or capsules of fertiliser that last a whole season. These are great and they really do work. Take your pick.

Pruning

Because most kinds of tree fruits are going to be grown as dwarf pyramids, the greater part of the pruning will be done during the summer and not in the winter.

To form a dwarf pyramid after winter planting, if you are starting with a dormant one-year-old (maiden) tree, cut the central stem back to 20in (50cm) high. All side-shoots longer than 6in (15cm) are then shortened to 5in (13cm). Shorter ones are left alone. In the following winter, the new growth on the central leader is cut back to

8–10in (20–25cm) and the new growth on laterals (side-shoots) to 6–8in (15–20cm). From then on, winter pruning is confined to shortening back the central leader as before; side-shoots are dealt with in the summer as follows.

In late July or early August, when the growth has stopped, the leading shoots on the branches (branch leaders) are shortened to 5–6in (13–15cm). Side-shoots arising directly from the branches are cut back to 3in (8cm) and those from previously pruned side-shoots to 1in (2–3cm).

This routine is carried out every winter and summer until the tree reaches the desired height, after which the central leader is treated as a side-shoot.

Overwintering

All hardy fruits must be overwintered outdoors with the pots plunged in peat, sand or straw to stop them getting frosted and possibly broken. It also protects the rootball from any intense cold. An alternative is to bury the pots in a trench in a spare piece of ground but there may be the problem of worms entering the compost in the pots through the drainage holes. The whole point about leaving the plants outside during the winter is that they need a certain amount of low temperature treatment in order to fruit properly. If you keep them in the greenhouse over the winter 'to be kind', you will simply reduce their fruiting capacity. Most are perfectly hardy and need the cold to operate properly.

In fact, fruit trees should only be brought into the greenhouse when it is going to benefit them; at other times they should be in a sheltered and sunny position outside. The time for housing them will, of course, vary with the kind of fruit. The really hardy types, such as apples, pears, plums and cherries, should only come under cover at the times already mentioned. Grapes, figs and peaches etc., the slightly less hardy fruits, can also benefit from greenhouse conditions when the fruit is ripening towards the end of the summer. At this time, they need all the sun and warmth they can get to ripen and mature properly so that their full flavour is developed.

Having said that, it is a good idea to bring the trees in at night when in blossom to protect them from any frost and also on wet and miserable days. This, though, raises the question of pollination.

Pollination

Obviously a few bees and insects are going to find their way into the greenhouse, but there are seldom enough to guarantee effective pollination if the weather is poor for days on end. Most trees will need to be hand pollinated.

There is nothing difficult about this as it merely involves transferring pollen from the male anthers of the flowers to the female stigma. This is achieved very simply with an artist's soft paintbrush. You still see some writers recommending a rabbit's tail instead of a brush, but this is only a relic of a bygone age; a soft brush is perfectly adequate and does an excellent job. Choose a warm and sunny day for the hand pollination; you will find that more pollen is released then.

Keep the trees under cover for a few days after the petals have fallen to make sure that fertilisation has taken place, then they can be moved outside again.

Rootstocks

Mention has already been made about the different rootstocks on which certain tree fruits are grown and how these will affect the vigour and ultimate size of the trees. There are, therefore, definite rootstocks which are favoured for pot culture.

A short list of the most suitable rootstocks for the different kinds of fruit, together with some of the best varieties might, therefore, be helpful.

Apples – Rootstocks M26 and MM106.
Cookers are on the whole less suitable than dessert varieties because of their usually greater vigour, but Lane's Prince Albert (cooker) is naturally dwarf and spreading.

Pears – Rootstock Quince C if available, Quince A if not.
Louise Bonne is particularly good for its quality and Concorde for its reliability.

Plums – Rootstock Pixy.
Early Transparent gage, Reine Claude de Bavay and Denniston's Superb are all top quality desserts, but grow Victoria for its reliability if you want to play safe.

Cherries – Rootstock Colt.
Stella is a reliable self-fertile variety so is the best choice for gardens.

Peaches – Rootstock St Julien A.
Peregrine is the hardiest variety and suitable for outdoors. Royal George is a good late variety that should be ripened under cover if the summer is poor.

Nectarines – Rootstock St Julien A. Grow Lord Napier.

Apricots – Rootstock St Julien A.
Moorpark is the traditional variety, but there are two from Canada: Farmingdale and Alfred.

Figs – Grown in their own roots.
Brown Turkey is the standard variety, but Negro Largo is higher quality though definitely needs a greenhouse.

Grapes – Grown on their own roots.
Black Hamburgh and Muscat of Alexandria (white) should both be grown in the greenhouse, though Hamburgh will succeed outside on a warm wall in the south.

Let us now consider the cultivation of some fruits that are more on the exotic side.

Figs

It is perfectly easy to grow figs outdoors, particularly against a sunny wall or fence, but they do a great deal better under glass and far superior varieties can be used. There are two ways of going about it: they can either be grown in pots or in the greenhouse border. Pot culture really only has one thing against it; you have to spend more time watering in the summer. The advantages, though, are overwhelming. You have far more control over the growth of the tree, it takes up much less room and it is certain to carry more fruit than a similar-sized tree in the border.

A 9 or 10in (23–25cm) pot is fine, but a rather different compost to that suitable for other fruit plants is required because, if it is a touch too rich, the fig will simply explode into growth at the expense of fruit. For this reason, John Innes Seed compost does well, provided that the drainage is improved with some pea-sized mortar rubble.

When potting, firm the compost down really well both below and around the roots so that they have to fight for everything that they need. Repotting every other year is normally quite enough and should be done as follows.

After leaf-fall, take the tree out of the pot, loosen the roots a little and cut them back so that there is a gap of about ½ in (1.25cm) around the rootball when the tree is replaced in the pot. Fill up firmly with fresh compost and forget about it for another two years.

In the autumns when you are not repotting, just loosen the top 3–4in (75–10cm) of compost and replace it with fresh.

Depending on the amount of heat available (and its cost), early March is the earliest feasible time to start the trees into growth and, by doing it then, you will still get two crops a year: one in the early summer and the other in about September. A temperature of 55–60°F (13–16°C) is needed to get the plants going and they must have full light the whole time. Once the foliage is growing nicely, the temperature can be allowed to rise to about 80°F (27°C). At that point, keep the air and the compost moist with plenty of water and feed about once a month with a tomato liquid feed (high potash).

During the spring and early summer, new shoots must be stopped at five leaves to encourage more to develop; it is this second generation of shoots that carry the autumn crop.

Negro Largo, as already mentioned, is one of the best for indoors with Bourjassotte Grise as an alternative. Read's Nursery of Lodden, Norfolk, list them both; they are the leading nursery for greenhouse fruits.

Oranges and Lemons

Oranges and lemons can also be grown more or less anywhere that has sufficient light and heat and, in many ways, sunroom extensions are ideal as you can enjoy the beautifully scented flowers.

We will deal just with oranges, but all other citrus fruits follow along the same broad lines.

Once again, there is the choice between pots and borders and, once again, pots are the better of the two. Choose a size in proportion to that of the plant and make sure that the drainage holes are adequate; none of these tropicals and subtropicals can stand a hint of waterlogging. A reliable brand of John Innes No. 3 is as good a compost as any.

The pots can be moved onto a warm and sunny patio during the period June–August.

Let us start with their cultivation in winter. Oranges will survive at any temperature above freezing, but, remember, the lower the temperature, the less water they will need and no feed at all. They will start growing in March or April and will come into flower in the summer; the resulting fruitlets pass through the winter small and green. This is normal as they will continue to grow with the arrival of the warmer weather and will ripen in the summer.

Throughout the growing season water must be given freely, with overhead spraying on hot days to maintain a moist atmosphere. This should be stopped on warm days when the trees are in flower as scorching can result. A general liquid feed will be needed, starting off fortnightly and increasing with the growth rate to weekly, but returning to fortnightly towards the end of the summer.

Oranges need no regular pruning. Simply maintain the shape of the bush and check any new shoot that is getting out of hand.

Scale insects, mealy bugs and the ubiquitous greenfly are the main pests.

When propagating, pips are fun and free, but seldom give rise to a variety similar to the parent. It is far safer to take heel cuttings about 6in (15cm) long from existing plants in early autumn; give them plenty of bottom heat. Malta Blood and St Michaels are good varieties, but Ruby Blood reigns supreme. All are available from Read's.

Pineapples

It may appear to be moving from the sublime to the ridiculous, but, if you can maintain a minimum night temperature in the greenhouse during the winter of 60–65°F (15–18°C), you might be able to grow pineapples.

However; you will also need to keep the temperature at 70–75°F (21–24°C) by day in the winter with a night minimum of the same during the growing season. Along with this, the temperature variation should be kept to about 10°F (5–6°C) if possible, though, in the summer, up to 100°F (38°C) is tolerable for short periods.

The compost required by pineapples is nowhere near as exotic as the citrus fruits; two parts of fibrous loam to one part of peat is quite suitable. The addition of some well-rotted manure or garden compost will make it even better. Above all, though, it must be free-draining, so never firm it down too much in the pots.

As with other bromeliads, watering and feeding should be kept to an absolute minimum in the winter, but it is hard to over-water pineapples in the spring and summer. During this period, a general liquid feed should be given monthly, but both this and the watering should be reduced when the fruit is ripening. Give as much light as possible at all times by keeping the plants close to the glass.

Any really serious pineapple grower in the UK will very probably build a special bed for the plants to fruit in, but this is not vital and a succession of pots, from a 4in (10cm) for the young plants up to about 9in (23cm) for fruiting in, is quite normal. For really big plants, you can even go up to a 12in (30cm) pot.

With the exception of greenfly, pests are much the same as for oranges.

The simplest way to start growing pineapples is to cut off and root the rosette at the top of a bought fruit. These can usually be twisted off quite easily and modern varieties have the advantage in that they are spineless. Tidy up the base of the 'cutting' with a sharp knife, give it a touch of rooting hormone powder or liquid and stand it in a 50/50 peat/sand mix or seed and cuttings compost. Err on the dry side at this stage as rooting will be quicker and there is less risk of a fungus rot setting in. You will probably find it hard to achieve, but a bottom heat of 90°F (31°C) should be aimed at.

Start the propagation in the spring so that the whole growing season lies ahead; at the end of which, the top should have rooted. Once rooted, pot it up and away you go. Plants can also be raised from seed, but, here again, a great amount of bottom heat is needed and the plant will take three to four years to reach fruiting size. Nothing need be done to encourage the plant to fruit; it will do so in its own good time, but there is this terrific heat requirement. Without it, success will be limited.

However, once a plant has fruited, you have the best propagating material of all because suckers arise from the base of the stem. These can be taken at any time from March to September, according to when the fruit was removed, but the larger they are, within reason, the more likely they are to root. Pull off the suckers, tidy up the base, pull a few of the lowest leaves off, dip the base in rooting compound and stand them in the compost so that just the base of the lowest leaves are covered. A propagator is a handy tool for rooting.

As you can see, heat is the main need if pineapples are to be grown successfully, but, given this, they are not too hard.

Ripley Queen and Smooth Leaved Cayenne are the varieties most likely to give good results.

9 Fruit Reference Section

Now that we have had a look at the background and the main considerations that have to be borne in mind as regards fruit growing at home, it's time to look at the individual fruits that you are likely to want to grow.

In many cases, mention has already been made of different kinds and aspects so this part of the book acts as a quick reference section and a safety net so that anything which has been left out can now be covered.

The subjects to come under discussion will include recommended varieties, suitable tree forms, the most appropriate pruning systems, the worst pests and diseases and anything else of importance.

Tree Fruits

APPLES

Apples are easily the most widely cultivated tree fruit in the UK, both by fruit farmers and private gardeners, From the enormous number of varieties which are generally available, here are some of the best for gardens.

One thing which will probably strike you as being particularly odd is the fact that Cox's Orange Pippin has been left out. This is intentional. It is a very unreliable cropper and is susceptible to all the major pests and diseases. It is not the sort of apple that should be grown by anyone new to fruit growing. In fact, the only good point about Cox is its superb flavour and quality. The best system is to buy Coxes apples when you want them and grow a much easier and more reliable variety at home, for instance Sunset. There is now a self-fertile clone of Cox that is indistinguishable from the original, but is much easier to grow. It grows and crops well in North Yorkshire whereas the original Cox's Orange Pippin was impossible.

Bramley might also have been omitted a few years ago on account of its tree size. Even on a dwarfing rootstock it needs careful growing to keep it in check. However, M9 and the much more dwarfing M27 rootstocks have made it possible to grow quite small and manageable trees.

Both varieties have substitutes of almost equal quality and of infinitely better character.

Dessert Varieties (Eaters)

Discovery August/September. Bright red. An excellent early apple that is fast replacing Worcester Pearmain both in orchards and in gardens. It is rather slow to come into bearing, but has good fruit size in a warm growing season. The fruits last much longer after picking than do those of Worcester. It is a moderately vigorous tree and crops well on fruiting spurs so is fine for the more intensive tree forms. Cox, Spartan and Greensleeves are good among the pollinators.

Fortune September/October. Striped red. This first-rate apple has Cox as one parent. The flavour is good and the texture juicy. It is a variable cropper, being good in some years and bad in others. Usually does best in the south and east. Of moderate vigour and producing a fairly upright tree. Inclined to bruise rather easily so the fruit isn't often seen for sale.

Sunset November/December. Very similar to, and a child of, Cox and certainly the variety to grow in gardens in place of it for a Cox-like flavour. The fruit tends to be on the small side for commercial growers, so is seldom grown. This, however, is of no consequence in a garden. A good spur-bearing variety and a tree of moderate vigour, upright and spreading.

Spartan October–February. Dark red, good flavour. A heavy cropping Canadian variety which sometimes needs thinning to maintain a good fruit size. A moderately vigorous, upright and spreading tree. Not the best garden variety because, although the flavour is good, the texture and skin are a little tough for British taste. Susceptible to apple canker.

Ashmead's Kernel November–March. Excellent and true russet flavour. A very old variety that keeps into March. Makes a fairly compact tree suitable for gardens.

Egremont Russet October/November. The main commercial russet variety and very popular. The amount of russet on the fruits varies enormously, but there should normally be about a 50 per cent coverage. The texture

is rather dry, but the flavour is characteristically nutty. Reasonably reliable cropper and suitable for intensive tree forms.

Ellison's Orange September/October. Liable to carry fruit only in alternate years (biennial cropping) if allowed to; prevent this by thinning the crop in an 'on' year. Juicy and with a slight aniseed flavour, but not widely grown commercially because it bruises very easily. Fairly resistant to spring frost Cox is one parent.

Greensleeves October/November. A new variety from East Malling Research Station aimed at the multitude of people who like a green eating apple, but who can't stand the sight or taste of Golden Delicious. It makes a compact tree that crops well from early in its life. Egremont Russet is a good pollinator. A great favourite of mine, but rather susceptible to apple scab in a damp year.

Kent November–January. Mainly red; juicy and aromatic.

Kidd's Orange Red November-January. A New Zealand apple with Cox as a parent. Cox-like flavour and a regular and heavy cropper with a nice looking half-russeted skin finish. Slightly more vigorous than Cox.

Rosemary Russet November–March. An old and excellent late keeping apple. Very rich flavour and of only moderate vigour. Unfortunately, and as is often the case with old varieties, reliability and cropping are not as good as one might hope for.

Cookers

Early Victoria (Emneth Early) July/August. The earliest cooker and should be grown far more in gardens because it crops at a time when the new season's cookers are expensive to buy. A longish apple of typical codlin shape; medium sized. A reliable and quite heavy cropper that responds excellently to intensive growing as fruiting spurs are formed readily. One of the few varieties that is best spur-pruned (see page 60). Keswick Codlin is very similar to it.

Golden Noble   October–December. Principally a garden variety. Does not form spurs readily, so best grown as a lightly pruned bush tree. Excellent cooker that fluffs up a treat. Medium to large; yellow when ripe.

Grenadier   August/September. The earliest popular cooker and the one most grown in gardens and commercially. A slow grower; but a regular cropper. A good pollinator for Bramley. Medium to large fruits with slight colour. Beautiful cooker that breaks up well.

Lane's Prince Albert   December–March. Small and compact tree, first-rate for gardens and for growing in containers. Spurs produced very freely. Susceptible to mildew, but quite resistant to scab so well suited to the wetter West. Fruit holds together well on cooking, so good for baking. My alternative to Bramley.

Howgate Wonder   November–March. A heavy and regular cropper that keeps well. Very large fruit which break up well when cooked. Produces spurs readily. Moderately vigorous and upright, later spreading. A wonder indeed. Capable of producing enormous fruits that can weigh nearly 4lb (1.8kg).

It has been mentioned from time to time that apples can be grown as cordons and espaliers. Both these tree forms need the support of wires. They may, though, be grown either against a wall or fence or in the open garden. Cordons are more commonly grown in the open, espaliers against a wall or fence.

For cordons, 9ft (2.7m) long posts should be driven into the ground so that a good 2ft (60cm) is buried; they should be 12ft (3.6m) apart. Three horizontal wires are attached to the posts; the lowest 30in (75cm) above the ground, the next 2ft (60cm) higher and the top one 2ft (60cm) above that. To these wires are fastened canes, approximately 9ft (2.7m) long, at an angle of forty-five degrees. It is to these canes, not the wires, that the trees are tied.

The arrangement of wires for espaliers is slightly more extensive due to the nature of the training and the size of the tree. The height to which an espalier can be allowed to grow is governed by the height of the wall, fence or posts. For this last, the posts should be the same as for cordons.

The horizontal wires are normally stretched 1ft (30cm) apart, but this can be reduced to 9in (23cm) (three courses of bricks), provided that you keep the fruiting spurs smaller.

The most common and popular way of growing apple trees has always been as bush trees pruned either on the regulated or, preferably, the renewal system. Some varieties, such as the cooker Early Victoria and the dessert variety Miller's Seedling, respond better to spur pruning in which all new shoots not wanted as branches or extension growth are cut back to 2in (5cm) in the winter; the new growth on the branch leaders are cut back to half their length.

One of the most recently introduced tree forms is the spindle bush shape. This requires a minimum of pruning and, although this doesn't produce a very pretty tree, being rather more straggly than most people want to see in a garden, it does induce bearing early in the tree's life and heavy crops are carried.

As regards the problems of pests and diseases, here are some of the most common, along with the best ways of dealing with them.

Pests

Capsid bugs Small punctures in leaves and fruit leading to distorted growth. Spray the tree with systemic insecticide before and after blossom.

Caterpillars Usually worst in April/May. Holes eaten in flower buds and leaves. Spray with contact insecticide when first seen and repeat as necessary.

Codling moth Pink maggots in fruit from July onwards. Spray with contact insecticide in mid-June and three weeks later.

Greenfly Active from before blossom until late summer. Spray with systemic insecticide whenever seen.

Red Spider Mite Pale, stippled markings on leaves with tiny yellow or orange mites and webbing underneath. Leaves may become bronzed. Spray with systemic insecticide fortnightly from fruitlet stage.

Apple Sawfly White maggot in fruitlets in June. Fruitlets drop. Spray with contact insecticide at petal fall.

Woolly Aphis Cotton wool-like colonies on twigs and branches. Spray with systemic insecticide.

Diseases

Canker Rough and cracked lesions in bark on branches and shoots. Remove small branches if badly diseased; pare off bark with a knife and paint with a suitable canker paint, such as Medo.

Mildew New shoots and blossom trusses covered with powdery white fungus. Pick off infected parts if only minor attack. Spray all infected trees with systemic fungicide when first seen and fortnightly thereafter.

Scab Starts as black spots on leaves and then fruitlets. Later, cracks appear on fruit lesions. Spray with systemic fungicide as for mildew.

Storage Rots Spray in late July and twice more at three-week intervals before picking with systemic fungicide.

PEARS

In nearly all respects the cultivation of pears is the same as for apples. The tree forms and shapes are the same, i.e. standards and half-standards, bush trees, cordons and espaliers. However, the pruning of the large and 'extensive' types of tree (standards, half-standards and bush trees) is rather different. Although the renewal system is suitable in principle, it does tend to produce a more rigid tree which grows taller and less spreading than do apples. For this reason, the regulated system, with a touch of the renewal brought in to keep th e trees young, is best for them. The pruning of pears was beautifully summed up many years ago by one of the leading commercial growers; he recommended that you 'leave them judiciously alone'. In other words, do as little to them as you have to.

Although there are a good many pear varieties available, most unfortunately those that are grown in gardens are largely confined to three; Williams, Conference and Comice. This is a great shame because Williams has a terribly short season when it is in good condition, the flavour of Conference leaves quite a lot to be desired in any but a good summer and Comice, though of the finest quality, makes a huge tree that crops rather unreliably.

Eaters

Beth September. Excellent for gardens. This is an English-bred variety that lay dormant and unintroduced for many years because of its unsuitability for commercial growers. The reason for this unsuitability? Its shape is inclined to be variable, so it doesn't look nice in the greengrocer's. That may be a valid reason, but it shouldn't be allowed to influence gardeners.

Onward Late September–early. October Another first-rate new English variety. It has Cornice as one parent. It also was rejected at first because of its short shelf-life but, as with Beth, this needn't worry gardeners.

Beurre Superfin September/October. Very high quality dessert pear raised in France. This would normally mean that it only crops moderately well in the cooler UK climate, but this variety crops quite well and is of superb quality. Pick it in late September and eat it before it becomes soft.

Conference October/November. Fair flavour, but a regular and heavy cropper, which can make up for its lack of excellence. Conference is capable of setting fruit from its own pollen, and even without fertilisation, but it still produces its heaviest crops when cross-pollinated.

Doyenne du Comice November. The very highest quality pear, but not all that easy to grow well as it really needs the protection of a warm wall to give of its best. A strong grower. A 'must' if you want perfection.

Cookers

Catillac A very late cooking pear that can still be used in April. The best cooker. People who sometimes have a pear tree in their new garden whose fruit never seems to soften and ripen have usually got Catillac. This is perfectly normal behaviour for the variety and is desirable in a cooker.

Although pears are remarkably similar to apples in so many cultural respects, they do have one distinct advantage; they get very many fewer pests and diseases. The most common are capsids, caterpillars and greenfly, with scab being the worst disease. The controls are as for apples.

PLUMS AND GAGES

Although an extremely popular and delicious fruit, plums have the disadvantage of being unreliable as regards cropping. Flowering early in the spring (mainly March), they run the risk of having the blossoms frosted. Another snag attached to this early flowering is that pollinating insects, such as bees, are most reluctant to venture out into what is normally, at that time of year; a bitter east wind. For these reasons, plums are not often grown extensively in gardens.

Plant plum trees in a warm and sheltered position. If the garden is particularly cold and nowhere in it is suitable, then perhaps you ought to think again before planting plums.

While the trees are small, the best frost protection is simply to spread some horticultural fleece or some polythene over them on evenings that look likely to develop into frost.

Plums in rural areas may have the added hazard of bullfinches feeding on the buds in a harsh winter.

Perhaps it would be useful to have a quick word here about the difference between plums and gages. Though more of academic interest than horticultural accuracy, the traditional classification is that gages are for eating and plums for cooking. Today, the emphasis is much more on dual-purpose varieties that crop heavily and, for the modern small gardens, this makes a lot of sense.

Plums can be grown as standards, half-standards, bush trees, pyramids and fan-trained trees. Unless you want a traditional large tree, make sure that you buy one that is growing on the rootstock Pixy. This produces a tree about two-thirds of the normal size.

Although fans may be grown trained to wires or canes in the open garden, it is more usual for them to be trained to a wall or fence. The horizontal wires for training the fans should be 6in (15cm) apart, or two courses of bricks.

New varieties appear from time to time, but none of them exhibit any great advantage over those that we already have. For that reason, Victoria is still the most widely grown variety, both commercially and in gardens, and there really seems to be no reason for changing. There is no other plum that can match it for reliability, ease of growing, flavour, and crop weight. Others are better than Victoria in one respect or another, but none overall.

From the many available, here are some of the best garden varieties.

Czar   late July – cooking – purple

Opal   early August – dual purpose – dark purple

Oullin's Gage   early August – dessert – golden

Denniston's Superb   mid-August – dessert – green/yellow

Early Transparent Gage   mid-August – dessert – green

Cambridge Gage   late August – dessert – green

Victoria   August – dual-purpose – bright red

Marjorie's Seedling   late September – cooking – purple

Victoria is one of the best self-fertile varieties, but, even so, does not carry what it is capable of unless cross-pollinated. Other self-fertile varieties include Denniston's Superb, Czar Early Transparent, Oullin's Gage, Marjorie's Seedling and Merryweather damson.

Cambridge Gage is partially self-fertile, but Coe's Golden Drop and the Old English Greengage must be cross-pollinated to produce any fruit.

Denniston's Superb and Coe's go well together; Czar, Victoria and Merryweather damson also do and so do Old English Greengage and Marjorie's Seedling.

Plums like a soil that is not too chalky or limey as these are apt to turn the leaves yellow (through lack of iron and manganese) and reduce the crops. Strongly acid soils are equally unsuitable as calcium is in short supply.

Pests and diseases can also be troublesome. The worst is usually a greenfly attack from midsummer onwards; use a systemic insecticide against them the moment you see any. The most noticeable place is going to be on the end of the current season's new shoots where colonies of the Mealy Plum aphid soon stunt the growth.

There is also a little moth (the Red Plum Maggot) that is responsible for maggots in the plums. The best control for this is a thorough spraying with a contact insecticide during June. The actual time can be determined with the help of a specific pheromone trap which should be hung in the tree(s) in late May.

Brown Rot is probably the worst disease; this can be kept in check, but not really cured, with a fortnightly systemic fungicide spray during the summer. The other symptom to look out for are the infected fruits remaining on the trees during the winter. All these should be picked off and burned. They are easily recognised as shrivelled, brown and with fungal spores on the outside.

Another bad disease, Silver Leaf, can only be controlled by cutting back all infected branches into unstained wood during the summer. Infected branches are easily spotted because their leaves are pale green and have a silvery sheen to them. Summer is also a good time to carry out ordinary pruning because it is the time of year when cuts, especially saw cuts, seal themselves very quickly, thus preventing entry of the disease spores.

Actually, once the main framework of branches has been formed in the first four to five years, the pruning of plum trees is really just a question of keeping them tidy and free from dead, diseased, damaged and badly placed branches. No detailed

attention is needed, unless you are growing fan-trained trees against a wall.

Fertiliser treatment is much the same as for other fruit trees in that it should be applied in the late winter so that it is washed down to the roots before growth starts in the spring. The type to use is also as for other fruit trees, that is one with a comparatively high potash content. 'Growmore' is better than most because it has a nitrogen, phosphate and potash content balanced equally at 7 per cent each.

The traditional way of growing plums is as standards, half-standards and bush trees. These are large trees whose trunks alone are 6ft (1.8m), 4ft (1.2m) and 2ft (60cm) tall respectively. Of these, only bush trees are really suitable for gardens.

As with apples and pears, plums can also be grown in a restricted form. The shaping is called 'festooning' because, rather then cutting the young main shoots back, they are pulled hard over and tied to lower branches in late summer after growth has stopped for the year. They can also be fan-trained to canes in the open garden or against a wall. In the latter case, wires are run along the wall 6in (15cm) apart.

The training of a fan is as follows.

1st February (after planting as one-year-old tree) Cut it back after planting to 24in (60cm) high.

1st summer Retain only two side-shoots. These should be opposite each other and 9–12in (23–30cm) from the ground. When 18in (45cm) long, tie them to the wires at forty-five degrees and remove the central stem above them. Remove any other shoots as they appear.

2nd February Shorten the two shoots to 18in (45cm) long.

2nd summer Retain the extension growth and two new shoots on the upper surface and one on the lower of the two original side-shoots. Remove all others as they appear.

3rd February Cut back each of the eight new shoots to 2ft (60cm) long.

3rd summer Treat each of the eight shoots as last summer according to the available room on the wall. If there isn't enough room, restrict the number of new shoots accordingly. Thereafter, the main concern is to prune and train for fruit, the basic framework of the tree having been created. Any shoots required for filling in gaps can be left but all others are stopped when they have made six or seven leaves.

Once the fruit has been picked, the shoots that were previously stopped are cut back by half.

Fortunately, it all sounds more complicated than it really is.

CHERRIES

Until quite recently, the idea of growing sweet (dessert) cherries in gardens was not only questionable, it was almost considered idiotic. They made huge trees, were irregular croppers and special provisions had to be made for cross-pollination.

The situation has changed somewhat in recent years, however, because we now have rootstocks that are producing smaller trees and self-fertile varieties of sweet cherry that make cross-pollination desirable rather than vital. This one variety that will set a good crop with its own pollen is Stella. The combination of Stella growing on the semi-vigorous rootstock Colt is the largest tree worth considering for gardens.

Even more recently the continental rootstock Gisela has become available in the UK. If all goes well, we should be able to have sweet cherry trees no more than 6–10ft (1.8–3m) high.

Morello is the best known acid cherry. It makes a neat free-standing tree that is easily grown in small gardens. It will grow and fruit well when fan-trained against a wall, even a north-facing one, the wire system being the same as for plums.

PEACHES AND NECTARINES

When one considers growing peaches or nectarines at home, some authorities will tell you that there is the choice between growing them as bush trees in the open and as fan-trained against a wall.

It is perfectly true that peaches have been grown outdoors as bush trees successfully; the Suffolk fruit farmer and author, the late Justin Brook, grew them commercially as bush trees for some years. For most of us, though, it is far too risky a pastime and they need the shelter and warmth of being trained against a sunny wall or fence.

The main problem is the peaches' natural habit of flowering in what could, in some years, be the depths of winter; sometimes as early as February in a mild year. Couple this with the fact that they are difficult to ripen in the average British summer and you will see why they need that protection.

Stick to growing them trained against a sunny wall and you will make a success of them. The way to train them is akin to that described for plums, but there are certain important differences. For a start, you must make sure that it is a wall that receives plenty of sunshine; this means one facing south or west. With an aspect of that sort, not only will the shoots and fruits receive ample sunshine to ripen them properly, but the wall will itself retain heat during the day and release it at night.

The best method of training is undoubtedly as a fan. This is best for all stone fruits (plums, cherries, peaches etc.) whereas, as we have already seen, apples and pears are normally grown as espaliers.

A two to three-year-old tree that has already been started as a fan is the best buy. It will cost a bit more than buying a maiden tree, but it saves a couple of years of training and also means that you'll get fruit that much sooner.

However, for the sake of completeness, let us start from scratch with a maiden. After planting, the main central stem is cut back to a side-shoot growing from a point about 2ft (60cm) from the ground.

During the following summer, more growths will appear from the main stem. Choose and retain two of these, one on each side, that are about 9in (23cm) from the ground and pinch off all the others. These two will be permanent branches and should be tied to canes set at forty-five degrees.

When they are about 18in (45cm) long, the central stem and its side-shoots are cut away and the two are left to grow on. Both these are cut back to 18in (45cm) in the late winter.

When new shoots growing from these the following summer are about 4in (10cm) long, three or four from each that are growing in the same plane as the wall (not growing at it or away from it) are retained and tied in.

This process of selecting and tying in during the summer and shortening to encourage branching in the winter is carried on until the allotted space is filled. If all of this sounds too complicated to be true, see the diagram on page 58 – it says it all.

We can, though, allow some fruits to form during this building process without overtaxing the tree. The important thing about peaches is that, unlike apples and pears, the fruit is produced on the previous year's growth. Once the first foundation branches have been retained and tied in, start to think about fruit production. This really consists of retaining temporary fruiting shoots on the permanent branch system.

During the spring, many new shoots grow from the tied-in branches and shoots; these will bear the next year's crop. Of these, only the ones growing from the top or bottom surface of the branch/shoot are retained. Even all these cannot be allowed to stay without causing overcrowding, so they are thinned to about 6in (15cm) apart along both surfaces.

They are tied in towards the end of the summer and, should any exceed 18in (45cm) long, the tips are nipped out. This pinching out and tying in continues each spring and summer.

Once the tree is fruiting, the fruited shoots need attention. This is quite simple because, if there is room for a fruited shoot to be kept as a branch, then it is tied in. If not, then it is cut back to the little cluster of buds at the base.

The list of available varieties suitable for growing outdoors is small. The three main criteria by which any fruit is judged are reliability, crop weight and flavour and one variety is seldom good in all three respects. However on balance, here are the best varieties in order of excellence.

Peregrine   (Early August)
Rochester   (Mid-August)
Duke of York   (Mid-July)
Lord Napier   (Early August) is the best nectarine.

A nectarine is simply a smooth skinned peach; botanically, they are the same. Even so, nectarines do seem to be less hardy and are not grown in the UK nearly as much as peaches are.

Incidentally, peaches and nectarines are seldom cross-pollinated as most people have a single tree. However, like nearly all fruits, they crop better if there is another variety nearby to pollinate them.

A point which often crops up in discussing fruit growing is the ease with which peaches can be grown from stones. The only problem is that, as with other kinds of fruit, there is no telling what quality of peach the resulting tree will produce. This is because, when grown from seeds, most fruits don't come true to type. However, it's great fun and perfectly easy to do and the new variety is often close to the parent in quality.

Opinions differ as to whether or not the seed should be removed from the stone, but on the whole, this is recommended because it can take years for the hard shell to break down sufficiently for the seed to germinate. It is better to saw the stone open carefully with a small hacksaw rather than trying to smash it open with a vice, which usually ends with the seed getting crushed as well.

Open the stone and sow the seed in the spring so that it has the whole growing season to germinate and grow. It can be sown either in a pot of seed compost in the greenhouse or window sill or in garden soil in the open; both ways are perfectly successful.

Seedling trees take longer to come to fruiting than budded or grafted ones so it may be five to six years before you see your first fruit. Have patience, though, it may well be worth it.

The most damaging disease attacks both peach and nectarine and also almond trees. It is peach leaf curl, a fungus disease that leads to characteristic red and distorted leaves. Spray with a copper fungicide in spring when the new shoots have just started to grow and again in the autumn when most of the leaves have fallen. Keeping the foliage dry by draping polythene over the trees during the spring and summer helps enormously in reducing the disease.

There is, in fact, a new peach variety called Avalon which is said to be resistant to peach leaf curl. If this proves to be correct and is long-lasting, it's a boon. An interesting point here is the difference between immunity and resistance. If Avalon has immunity from peach leaf curl, it means that it will not get it. If it has resistance to it, it can get it but is much less likely to.

APRICOTS

Apricots can perfectly well be grown in the UK, but they need to be fan-trained against a south or west wall to be successful.

Their cultivation is as for peaches and nectarines.

Oddly enough, even though fewer trees are grown here, up to nine varieties are offered for sale by Deacon's at Godshill on the Isle of Wight and Reads of London. Of these, Moorpark is the best known, but two new ones from America, Alfred and Farmingdale, are most promising. It is early days yet, however, and they may not prove to be as hardy as the English Moorpark.

FAMILY TREES

A type of tree that is very popular in the smaller gardens of today are what are called Family Trees. Each tree is of one kind of fruit but consists of, usually, three varieties; for example Cox/Grenadier/James Grieve apples.

Clearly these trees are very economical of space and, after a few years, they will carry a useful crop of each variety because the pollination 'cocktail' is tailor made.

The only point worth remembering about them is that attention has to be paid to the vigour of each variety so that the stronger ones are not allowed to dominate the tree at the expense of the others.

Remember also that not all varieties always need quite the same pruning for best results.

Apples, pears, plums and cherries are all available as family trees. Deacon's on the Isle of Wight do an incredible mixture of varieties and fruits, including two/three/ and four-variety trees and plum/peach, plum/nectarine and plum/apricot trees, even a peach/nectarine/apricot, so there is very little limit to the combinations.

FIGS

We have already covered the growing of figs in the greenhouse, but they are a perfectly easy crop outdoors as well, though it must be said that they are always better in the generally warmer and sunnier south.

They are also a much more popular fruit than in the past and this is probably just as much for the artistic quality of their leaves and branches as for their fruit. Indeed, most of us know the shape of the leaves a great deal better than the appearance of the fruit.

Several varieties of fig are available from nurseries, but the scene is dominated by Brown Turkey. This is perfectly hardy and produces fruit in the late summer and early autumn until the weather gets too cold.

Another good variety to grow outdoors is Brunswick. It has larger fruit and they are oval rather than pear-shaped. The flavour, though, is only moderate.

In spite of the fig being a native of the Mediterranean, the main thing we have to do when growing it in gardens in Britain is to curb its vigour. If it is allowed to grow unchecked, cropping will suffer. For that reason, grow it in a part of the garden where the poorest soil exists; though there must still be plenty of sunshine and shelter from strong winds.

For those gardeners blessed with good soil, the answer is to dig plenty of brick and mortar rubble into the planting position. Ideally, dig out a hole about a yard (metre) square and 2ft (60cm) deep. Line it with corrugated iron or planks and fill it with a mixture of soil and rubble. In this you plant the tree.

Any fertilisers should be low in nitrogen or they will simply encourage growth at the expense of fruit. If you can give the tree a mulch of garden compost or rotted manure each spring and a dose of tomato or rose fertiliser (both high in potash) every other spring, this is ample.

Even in the sunnier south, where it is easy enough to grow figs as unrestricted trees in the open garden, it is still better to have them loosely fan-trained against a sunny wall or fence. If properly tended, the tree need take up an area of no more than about 8ft (2.5m) square. In the cooler north, this is really the only sensible way of growing figs.

The important and rather odd thing to understand about figs is that the fruits form in one year, overwinter on the tree and then ripen in the next. This is complicated by the fact that the embryo fruits form in the axil of the leaves throughout the growing season, not just in the spring, as is the case with other and more conventional fruits.

However, it is only those fruitlets that form towards the end of the summer that we are interested in. The ones that develop earlier are too small to ripen in the same year but too far advanced and tender to stand the winter cold. These earlier fruitlets must be removed or they will discourage the formation of more later on in the season: the very ones that we want. Pick off the unwanted ones as soon as they are large enough to handle until about mid-August. This will result in one or two embryo fruits at the end of each new shoot by the winter.

A useful way of ensuring that you get a nice lot of young shoots and fruitlets, and essential with trained trees, is to stop all new shoots at five to six leaves until the end of June. During July, all the retained shoots are tied in to the wall or fence to form a rough fan shape.

Winter pruning is delayed until about April to take into account any winter damage that occurs to the shoots; even in favourable areas and with the trees trained, hard weather can take its toll.

If all this sounds rather complicated, have no fear; even neglected fig trees will grow well and will certainly carry a few fruits.

Soft Fruits

STRAWBERRIES

Like all fruits, strawberries should have a sunny position so that the fruit is properly

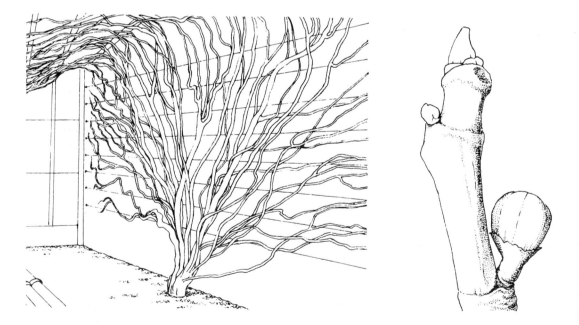

(Left) A fan-trained fig tree against the back wall of a lean-to greenhouse. A similar system may also be used in the open. (Right) Close-up of the tip of a fig shoot showing small embryo figs towards the top and also a larger one. The latter should be removed in the late summer.

ripened. Only then will the true flavour be brought out.

In most gardens, the vegetable plot is the most convenient place to grow them. For a start, the crop will be grown in rows and the row spacing is convenient for this. Secondly, strawberries seldom occupy the ground for more than three cropping seasons and this is frequently reduced to just one, depending on the variety.

Two to three dozen plants should normally be enough for the average family and remember that any surplus fruit can be frozen so there is unlikely to be any waste.

In spite of being relatively small plants, strawberries need good soil conditions. It should be deep, fertile and well drained. This can usually be achieved by digging in plenty of bulky organic matter, in the form of garden compost or well-rotted manure, in advance of planting.

The two main groups of strawberry are the summer (July) fruiting varieties and the Perpetual Fruiting sort that are normally induced to fruit only in the autumn. These latter are normally disbudded until the end of May so that they are prevented from wearing themselves out on early fruits.

A third group covers the tiny alpine varieties. These can be grown from seed, but the other two groups are propagated from runners.

Summer varieties should be planted during August or September if they are to give a good crop the following July. Perpetuals are planted from October to March; they will give a good first crop in their first year following planting at any time during this period.

The ground should be well prepared before planting strawberries with, as mentioned earlier; the incorporation of plenty of garden compost or manure. It should be firmed down well before planting and,

if the soil is reasonably fertile, no fertilisers will be needed at this stage.

The young plants will normally be growing in peat pots or blocks and the summer varieties should be planted firmly 15–18in (38–45cm) apart, depending on the standard of the soil and the vigour of the variety, with 30in (75cm) between rows.

Keep the plants well watered after planting so that they establish quickly. This helps to ensure a good first crop.

If, for any reason, planting is delayed beyond about the middle of September, the crop weight in the first summer will be progressively less the later that planting takes place. This can, to a great extent, be overcome by planting cold-stored runners instead of 'ordinary' ones. These can be bought and planted from May to mid-August and will fruit within two to three months, depending on the time of year.

The same planting rules apply to autumn varieties except that they are normally less vigorous and need only be 12–16in (30–40cm) apart in the row.

In the spring, when the first flowers are showing, straw should be spread beneath the plants to stop the fruits getting mud-splashed. Failing straw, special strawberry mats can be bought or made. There is even a type of slitted polythene that can be laid between the rows or, better still, lay this down before planting and plant through holes made in the planting positions.

After fruiting, it is wise to cut off all the foliage, flower stalks and runners (if they are not wanted for propagation). A lot of pests and diseases are removed with these and the plants quickly put out fresh and vigorous leaves to build up strength and fruit buds before the winter. Both the straw and the tops should go onto the compost heap. That done, give the plants a high potash feed to encourage them still further.

Ground covering is also needed for the perpetual (autumn) varieties, but the foliage should not be cut off after fruiting and it is normal to feed them in the spring rather than after fruiting. They are also improved if they are protected by cloches or polythene tunnels once the weather starts to deteriorate, usually towards the end of September.

As far as pests and diseases are concerned undoubtedly the worst problem is *Botrytis* (Grey Mould). This turns the fruits of all varieties into little grey balls of fluff and is particularly bad in a wet season. Spray every seven to ten days with a systemic fungicide once the first flowers are showing white.

Strawberries can also be forced in a greenhouse perfectly easily by bringing them in under cover at the end of February. Alternatively, first-year plants in the open can be cloched at the same time.

As an alternative to the open ground, strawberries may be grown in pots, proprietary Tower Pots, once-used growing-bags or in special strawberry barrels (wooden or clay). All have the advantage of mobility in case of frosts or simply for showing-off to neighbours by having them in fruit in a prominent position.

The best advice on varieties is to get in touch with a specialist nursery, such as Pomona Fruits of Walton-on-Naze, but here are some of the best and most popular.

Summer Varieties

Cambridge Favourite This has more than stood the test of time. It produces a lot of runners, is good for processing and will stay cropping well for maybe six years, provided that it stays healthy. The berries remain in good condition on the plant for several days after ripening.

Honeoye An early and popular variety. Large and round bright red fruits with very good, old-fashioned flavour. Heavy cropping. Excellent for jam. Fruit June to early July.

Alice A new variety showing good disease-resistance (excluding botrytis!). The sweet and well-coloured fruits have an excellent flavour. In season mid-June to late July.

Sonata This heavy-cropping, midseason variety could well rob Elsanta of the title of the most popular commercial variety. It is equally good for growing in gardens. The fruits are larger and sweeter than Elsanta and seem to be better able to withstand adverse weather, both wet and dry. Resistant to powdery mildew. Mid-June to mid-July.

Elsanta A very promising variety that ripens with Favourite. One of the best looking strawberries and gaining in popularity with commercial growers for the punnet trade. Moderate crops and with a flavour on a par with Vigour.

Hapil (Belgian) Taking over from Favourite on many commercial holdings. It will last for certainly four cropping seasons. The internal colour and flavour are better than Favourite. It is also firmer. Usually ripens just before Favourite and has a shorter, more condensed picking season.

Totem (Canadian) This is so far the best for any kind of processing. It's a firm berry and thaws well after freezing. It also has excellent internal colour; so makes a lovely jam. The flavour is good as well. Totem doesn't yield heavily so allow runners to root between the parent plants and form what is called a 'matted' row. Similar season to Favourite.

Everbearers

Aromel   The fruit is medium to large and with a good internal colour. Produces more runners than most other perpetuals. Very good flavour, but best grown for only one year. Crops from August to October.

Flamenco   A new, heavy-cropping variety of exceptional quality, with large and firm fruits. Very sweet and with excellent flavour. Resistant to verticillium wilt and powdery mildew. Season: August to October.

Malling Opal   A brand, spanking, new variety from the top fruit research station in England. It sets new standard for quality, flavour and yield amongst perpetuals. Heavy crops of large, sugar-sweet and juicy fruits. Season: August to October.

RASPBERRIES

Raspberries are probably second only to strawberries in their popularity as a garden fruit. They are easy to grow and any surplus can always be frozen. Their main disadvantage is that they take up a lot of room; not so much from the actual ground area but because of the shade that they create.

Varieties are either summer (July/August) or autumn (August to November) fruiting. The normal raspberries that you see in the shops are almost exclusively summer ones.

Summer Varieties

Glen Fyne   The newest one to appear from the Scottish Crop Research Institute at Dundee, the UK centre for summer raspberry breeding. It carries heavier crops than the widely grown Glen Ample. First

rate for both fresh fruit use and for jamming, etc. Its resistance to greenfly is good; therefore there is less risk of it contracting virus diseases. The fruits are large and sweet with a good 'shelf life'. Spine-free.

Glen Ample   The UK's most widely grown variety of summer raspberry. Heavy crops of large, well-coloured fruits with a good flavour. Spine-free.

Malling Admiral   Though from a previous generation, this is still an excellent late summer variety. Large, dark red fruits with an excellent flavour. Still well worth a place in any fruit garden. Not spine-free.

Malling Minerva   Another new one and regarded by some as the best of the early summer varieties. The berries have a very good flavour and readily part from the plug. Canes are spine-free and have a compact habit. Well worth a try. Late June to late July.

Tulameen   This has been around for some time now but is still regarded as 'new' to gardeners, although well known to commercial growers. The fruits are of high quality and yields are heavy. Nearly spine-free. Good frost resistance as the new canes are slow to emerge from the ground. Early July to early August.

Autumn Varieties

Autumn Bliss   Still the standard variety by which all others potentials are judged. The berries are firm with a very good flavour. The canes are relatively short and sturdy but still need the support of string run along each side of each row. I've regularly picked Autumn Bliss in November, even in North Yorkshire.

Allgold A new variety, which is a seedling or sport of Autumn Bliss (accounts vary) and similar to it in all respects except colour – it's bright yellow!

Polka Another new one with very heavy crops; said to be double those of Autumn Bliss. Also, shorter and sturdier canes. Starts fruiting two weeks earlier than Autumn Bliss. Mid-July to October. Spine-free.

Brice This is another very new one that was launched by Suttons Seeds. It is a Scotland-raised one that is still cropping well into November. Flavour is terrific, reminiscent of raspberry jam! Spine-free.

As one might expect, raspberries need sunshine for the fruits to ripen properly, to increase the sugar content and to bring out the true flavour. In addition, sunshine is required to ripen and mature the shoots so that ample and strong fruit buds are formed for the following year.

When to prune raspberries depends on whether they are the summer or the autumn varieties. The canes of the summer ones are produced during one year and they fruit in the following July/August. These varieties are pruned straight after fruiting by cutting right down to the ground those canes that have carried fruit. Immediately after pruning, the new canes are tied into the training wires so that they are spaced along the top wire every 4in (10cm). Preference must be given to the strongest and best canes and any that remain after tying in are cut out. In the spring, any canes growing higher than the top wire are shortened so that they don't extend more than 9in (23cm) above it.

The autumn varieties are annual; they grow and fruit in the same year. They are not cut down to the ground after fruiting, but are left until the following March to give some protection to the stools (plants) during the winter.

The summer varieties need a permanent support system, but the autumn do not. There are several different arrangements for the wires but the best for gardens is obviously going to be the cheapest and easiest to install. The wires need not be put up until growth has started in the spring after planting, but most gardeners like to get them up and ready beforehand.

A post is driven into the ground at each end of the row; these should be strutted for extra strength and, if they are further apart than about 12yds (11m), intermediate posts will be needed.

Two horizontal wires are stretched between the posts. The bottom one 2ft (60cm) from the ground and the top one 4ft 6in (135cm). Having two bottom wires, one each side of the post, makes life easier during the summer because the new canes can be trained up between them to hold them roughly in place before being properly tied in. When the time comes to tie in the canes, the two bottom wires are simply tied close together every 9–10ft (2.7–3m). The canes are then tied to the top wire so that they're about 4in (10cm) apart. Plant the canes 18–24in (45–60cm) apart.

Autumn raspberries only need support during the latter part of the summer when the canes are getting taller. A post is driven in at each end of the row and a length of stout twine is run between them down each side of the canes and drawn tight so that it holds them securely. The twine is normally left in position until the March pruning. Plant them 2ft (60cm) apart.

The width of the row of canes should be restricted to a maximum of 2ft (60cm). There should also be 2ft (60cm) clear between each row. Thus, you have 2ft wide rows with 2ft between each.

As regards pests and diseases, raspberries get their fair share, but the most serious are Grey Mould (*Botrytis*) and virus diseases. Grey Mould is always worst in a wet summer and spraying every seven to ten days with a systemic fungicide once the disease appears will be needed to keep it at bay.

Stunted, deteriorating and even dying canes indicate virus diseases. Dig up and burn the victims once the symptoms appear because there is no cure.

Spray regularly against greenfly before they can infect the canes with virus. Puckered and stunted tips to the shoots may also be caused by virus. Use a systemic insecticide against the greenfly.

Maggots in the ripe fruits are the larvae of the raspberry beetle. Spray with a contact insecticide when the first fruits are showing colour.

BLACKBERRIES AND THE HYBRIDS

Until quite recently, blackberries were hardly ever grown in gardens. The main problems were their size and vigour and the thorns. Although we still lack a dwarf blackberry, there are now several thornless selections and hybrids with less vigour. Added to that, the wild blackberries of the countryside have now disappeared to a great extent in the fetish for tidiness and a neat and ordered environment. Both these factors have encouraged people to grow blackberries in their gardens for themselves.

Although they can still take up rather a lot of room, this is only in respect of their length because they need to be trained to wires to make them easy to manage. In many cases, gardeners are now using them as fruitful and impenetrable hedges.

First, let us consider the varieties.

Himalaya Giant   Very vigorous and thorny. Large fruits. Mid to late season. Good flavour.

Loch Ness   Widely grown. Heavy crops of good quality, large fruits of good, but not exceptional, flavour. Much less vigorous than the older varieties. Thornless, therefore easy to train.

Waldo   Similar to Loch Ness, but with better-flavoured fruit. Thornless.

Black Butte   Brand new. Very large fruits up to 12gm in weight and 2in (5cm) long. Rich and sweet and full of flavour. Very winter hardy. Early July to mid August.

Oregon Thornless   Semi-vigorous and thornless. Medium fruits. Late. Good flavour.

Ashton Cross   Vigorous and thorny. Medium fruits. Midseason. Probably the best wild flavour of all.

Fantasia   A very new midseason vigorous and thorny variety with huge fruits and good flavour.

As a general rule, the thornless varieties crop lighter than the thorny. The life of a blackberry plant can be anything around twenty years.

Vigorous varieties should be planted 12–15ft (3.5–4.5m) apart; semi-vigorous, 10–12ft (3–3.5m).

The canes must be supported on horizontal wires stretched at 3, 4, 5 and 6ft high (1, 1.3, 1.6 and 2m) which are securely fastened to a stout post at each end of the row.

There are several recognised ways of training the canes and, although the 'weave' method is probably the best for ripening the fruit, it is hard to carry out with stiff blackberry canes. For this reason, the one or two-way rope systems are easier.

The illustration on page 41 shows the two-way system. For the one-way, the new canes are trained out and tied on one side only with the fruiting canes on the other.

Pruning is easy. The old fruited canes are simply cut out at ground level in the autumn after the fruit has been picked. The new canes are then tied in. Where new canes are in short supply, the old ones may be cut back to new canes that are growing from near their base.

Hybrid Cane Fruits

When we come to the hybrid cane fruits, the one that springs immediately to mind is the loganberry. This, like most of the others, is a hybrid between a blackberry and a raspberry, but being American in origin, these are not exactly the same as our own native ones.

The loganberry's main fault is its doubtful hardiness; a cruel winter can kill it almost to the ground. However, the fruit has excellent flavour, freezes well and makes good jam, even if its value for dessert is not particularly high.

The thorny variety LY59 has been largely replaced by the equal cropping, but thornless, LY654.

Loganberries should be planted at least 6ft (1.8m) apart and preferably 10ft (3m).

The much more recent tayberry was bred at the Scottish Crops Research Institute and is much better than the loganberry. Although its flavour and uses are similar; crop weights are double and it is much hardier.

Two types are available: the tayberry and the Medana tayberry. These are exactly the same in every respect except that the Medana prefix means that the plants have been tested for virus diseases and, as far as can be judged, found to be free. However, no reputable nursery would dream of selling possibly infected stock. Buckingham tayberry is a thornless version of the original. Tayberries should be planted 8ft (2.5m) apart.

The cultivation of tayberries is along very similar lines to that of the blackberry. They need the permanent post and wire support system and all operate the same biennial cropping with the canes growing one year and fruiting the next, after which they are cut out.

Even the pests and diseases are almost identical to those of raspberries.

GOOSEBERRIES

Of all the different bush fruits, gooseberries have traditionally been the most popular in gardens; and rightly so.

What other fruit takes up so little room compared to the crop it produces and whose fruits can be either cooked in the early summer or eaten fresh as dessert later on? They are also an extremely hardy fruit and this makes them especially popular in the north.

When gooseberries are grown as conventional bushes, plant them 5ft (1.5m) apart. Where space is limited, they can be grown as 'U' cordons. For these, the young bushes are planted 2ft (60cm) apart and are trained into two vertical arms 1ft (30cm) apart. They should be grown against fixed canes either in the open or against a wall or fence.

For best results the cordons should be summer pruned towards the end of June. This is done by shortening the new shoots back to 5–6in (12.5–15cm) so that more sun can reach the ripening fruits. Ordinary bushes benefit from this treatment as well.

Normal winter pruning should follow in November along the following lines.

Because gooseberries (and red currants) fruit best on spurs that form on the main branches, the first job is to create a branch system. After planting a young bush in the winter, therefore, retain just four or five strong shoots and cut them back to half their length; remove the rest. These pruned shoots will give rise to probably two more shoots each which, in the following winter; are treated similarly. Any other new shoots are cut back to about two buds.

Thereafter, all branch leaders are cut back by about a third and all other new shoots to two buds. This will soon build up a good branch system well furnished with fruiting spurs.

The worst pests of gooseberries are the caterpillars of the gooseberry sawfly. These will completely destroy the foliage if action is not taken against them. Spray with a contact insecticide in about mid-April when the caterpillars may first be seen. They can, though, appear at any time over the following two months so keep your eyes open.

The worst disease is American gooseberry mildew. This turns the young shoots white with fungus in the summer, but, even worse, it coats the fruits with a pale brown felt that makes them useless. Keep an eye open for this very serious disease and spray fortnightly with a mildew fungicide as soon as it is seen. The new variety Invicta is extremely resistant to mildew.

From the many varieties of gooseberry, the following are amongst those recommended for gardens.

Hinnonmaki Red   A new, mildew-resistant, dual-purpose variety.

Hinnonmaki Yellow   A new, mildew-resistant, dessert variety. Heavy crops of large, well-flavoured berries.

Invicta   Heavier crops and near immunity to mildew so a possible replacement for Careless. It grows into a large and thorny bush.

Leveller   The main commercial dessert variety. Good cropper and of first-rate flavour. Excellent in gardens, but needs good growing conditions.

Whitesmith   A good garden variety for dessert. Excellent flavour, but not as heavy cropping as Leveller.

CURRANTS

It seems that currants have always been something of the Cinderellas of the fruit world, where gardens are concerned. They are not often eaten as a fresh fruit but are some of the best there are for 'processing' in one way or another. There's red currant jelly to go with lamb instead of the rather acidic and overpowering mint sauce. Black currants are unrivalled as a supplier of vitamin C and make a lovely syrup. And I can personally recommend my own home made black currant gin. White currants are more of novelty value and are simply a colourless variety of the red currant.

A possible disadvantage of currants is the amount of room they take up in the garden. This is an unjustified complaint because there are several ways of growing them so that they take up next to no room at all.

In general, the growing of currants is perfectly simple.

Black Currants

Feeding is important for black currants. This is because the bushes are grown as stools and a continuous supply of new wood must be encouraged, as well as the crop itself. A good routine to get into is to apply a dressing of general fertilizer, such as Growmore, in the spring at the first sign of growth followed by a heavy mulch of garden compost or manure.

Black currants, in particular, are apt to shed their half-grown berries if they get too dry at the roots.

They must also be pruned correctly if they are to crop well. The general rule is to cut out branches once they are four years old. This is done as soon as the leaves start to fall in the autumn and is easily mastered by counting back the years of growth down a branch. They are easy to see as the wood gets darker with every year of age.

As regards varieties the new Ben Sarek and Ben Connan are likely to be the garden varieties of the future. They carry very heavy crops of large berries and, most important, are far less vigorous than other varieties and need only be planted 4ft (1.2m) apart instead of the usual 5–6ft (1.5–2m). Big Ben is all that you would expect it to be; heavy crops of huge berries. It is also resistant to mildew and leaf spot. It fruits in early July.

The latest flowering is Jet and this should certainly be grown where spring frosts are troublesome. Where not, Ben Sarek is much better.

Another good one, having taken over as the standard commercial variety, is Ben Lomond.

As regards ways of growing black currants, to reduce the amount of space they occupy, a simple solution is to prune out branches before they reach four years old. In fact, we can carry this a stage further and

emulate what was sometimes done commercially.

The system there is to treat a plot of black currants as two and, provided that the bushes are still young, cut down to the ground either one half of the area or alternate rows.

During the following year, the retained half will fruit while the cut-back ones will send up new shoots. In the autumn, the fruited bushes are cut to the ground while the others are left as they are. Come the summer; the 'young' bushes will carry a crop and the others will be growing. The former are then cut to the ground again. And so on, with any bush cropping every other year.

This is normally too wasteful of space for gardeners, but we can make use of the idea. All the bushes are cut down in the first place to set the system in motion, but, instead of cutting them back again straight after their first crop, they are allowed to grow on for another year when just the two-year-old branches are removed, together with any that are in the wrong place or damaged.

The result is a bush with two and one-year-old shoots fruiting and a younger lot growing. The system is simple and the currants can be planted about 2ft (60cm) apart to make a sort of hedge.

The worst problem likely to be encountered is Big Bud Mite, recognised by the large, pea-sized buds that appear once the leaves have fallen in the autumn. These fail to open, with obviously harmful results.

Equally bad is the Reversion virus disease that the mites spread from bush to bush. This causes a slow degeneration of the bushes with a dramatic reduction in crop. The only sure way to get rid of big bud mite and, therefore, reversion, is to dig up the infected bushes and burn them.

Red Currants

The cultivation of red (and white) currants is largely the same as that of gooseberries. They are grown as bushes on a short 'leg' and the aim should be to build up a branch system furnished with fruiting spurs.

The space-saving system for red and white currants is completely different to that for black currants as it involves the formation of cordon plants. The two shapes that are most commonly used are the single cordon and the 'U' or double cordon. Both are grown vertically and the only essential difference between them is the number of 'branches' that make up each bush.

The double cordon is more economical of plants but takes longer to cover the allocated area of wall or fence. The two arms are trained up canes or wires 1ft (30cm) apart and, where more than one plant is being grown, they are planted 2ft (60cm) apart. The method of pruning is exactly the same as for ordinary bushes in that all side-shoots are cut back to 1–2in (3–5cm) long in the autumn.

Besides the small amount of space occupied by cordons, they are also easy to protect from spring frosts and from birds eating the berries. You just throw some garden fleece over the bushes for the frost and a net for the birds.

Cordons, as well as conventional bushes, benefit from summer pruning in late June. All this involves is cutting all new side-shoots back to about 4in (10cm) long. The branch leaders are left until the early winter when they are shortened by about a third.

Red currants, too, have received a lot of attention as regards new varieties, many coming from the Continent.

Red Lake Now the main commercial variety and excellent for gardens.

Redpoll A new variety with very long strigs. An exceptional variety for the show-bench – it always wins!

Jonkheers van Tets A new early variety (late July) from Holland. Heavy crops on long bunches.

Redstart A brand new variety from East Malling Research Station in Kent and not yet generally available. Heavy crops excellent for red currant jelly. Worth waiting for.

White Versailles The standard white variety.

White Pearl An alternative white variety.

Red currants are pleasantly free of serious pests and diseases; greenfly are probably the most significant, unless you count birds. Blackbirds and thrushes will quickly strip the berries showing colour so netting or a chemical deterrent are needed.

GRAPES

Like many other fruits and vegetables, the growing of grapes in the UK has increased dramatically in recent years, mainly as a result of foreign travel and holidays abroad. However, the cultivation of dessert varieties outdoors is still something of a risky business; we just don't get enough sun to ripen the top quality dessert varieties. There are, though, some adequately hardy ones that can be grown outside in the UK without too much bother, but they could never be considered to be in the same class as the imported grapes. There are even commercial wine-grape vineyards in the UK now, some even as far north as Yorkshire.

The alternative is a greenhouse, where it is perfectly possible to mature high quality dessert varieties.

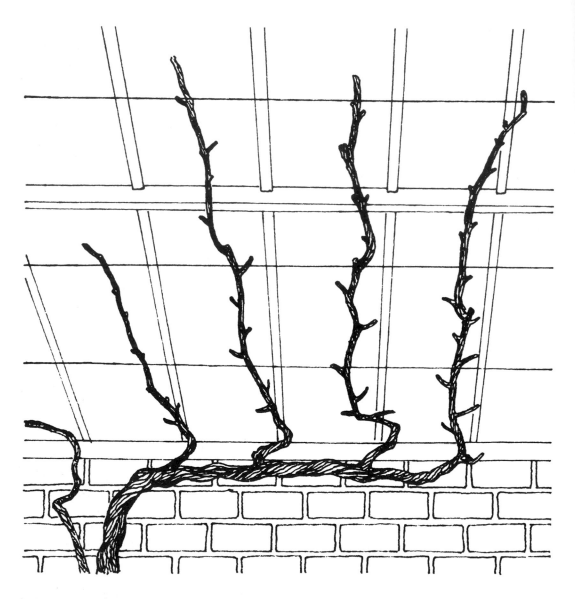

A vine in a greenhouse after winter pruning.

The dessert variety Black Hamburgh, normally regarded as the best for growing under glass in this country, also does quite well outdoors. However, this really only applies to the south and, even there, it should be grown against a south or west-facing wall.

Buckland Sweetwater is another greenhouse dessert grape that will crop reasonably well outdoors in the south in a good summer. Elsewhere and in a bad summer it's less reliable. Classified as 'white', it is a good variety with big bunches of large grapes when it does well. It's a vigorous grower, and rather susceptible to mildew.

Royal Muscardine, although possibly not top for quality, is certainly the best of those that are hardy and can be expected to grow well outdoors south of Lancashire/Yorkshire. The berries are white, quite large and of good quality with a Muscat flavour. However, the Rolls Royce of dessert greenhouse grapes is Muscat of Alexandria – once tasted, never forgotten.

The Strawberry vine is a smaller grape, pink and with a faint strawberry flavour. It comes from America and does very well in the south, but has a rather tough skin. It's possibly the hardiest of them all.

Turning to grapes to grow outdoors for wine production, one of the most successful in the UK is Triomphe d'Alsace. It ripens early, crops heavily and produces an excellent red wine.

Madeleine Angevine is also good and dual-purpose, making a passable dessert grape. It does quite well in the cooler districts. The fruit is pale green and ripens in early October.

Another good variety is Brant, or Brandt. This has small, black fruits and is a prolific cropper. As a bonus, the leaves often take on a good autumn colour.

One that gives an excellent quality wine is Muller Thurgau. It is a golden brown grape that ripens in mid-October.

A very popular one with amateurs is Seyve Villard 5276. It has regular and heavy crops which give a delicately flavoured wine.

Perlette is another dual-purpose variety, or rather triple-purpose as it's good for wine, for dessert and even for drying.

As most of us will be concerned mainly with greenhouse grapes, it would be as well to look at the pruning in some detail because, if it is neglected, the results can be a jungle.

It is very much a two-phase operation. The main pruning takes place in the winter when the plants are dormant; this is followed by trimming and tying in the newly grown rods in the summer.

It is very important that the rods are completely dormant when they are pruned or they will 'bleed' and this seriously weakens the plant. On average, Christmas is a good time and easy to remember.

After planting, the vine is cut back so that only a short length, 6in (15cm) or so, is left above ground; or inside the greenhouse, if the roots are outside.

In the late spring, shoots will grow from the stump, but no more than five should be kept. All others are pinched out as soon as possible. In the winter, the strongest shoot is cut back by half and the others are removed.

During the summer, the rod will develop side-shoots (laterals). With the exception of the top one, the leader, all are stopped (the tips are nipped out) when 2–3ft (60–90cm) long.

The leader is cut back in the winter to the point that is to be the permanent end of the vine rod. Any laterals that have grown on this top section are cut back to the buds at their base. Those lower down the rod, on the year older section, are cut back to about two buds from their base; this is usually about an inch (2–3cm).

Although only one shoot will be kept from these newly formed fruiting spurs, keeping two buds will allow you to choose the stronger of the two shoots that grow.

This method of training and pruning is called the vertical rod system and is the one normally used in a small greenhouse.

The same routine is carried out every year from then on, the canes that have fruited being cut back in the winter to two

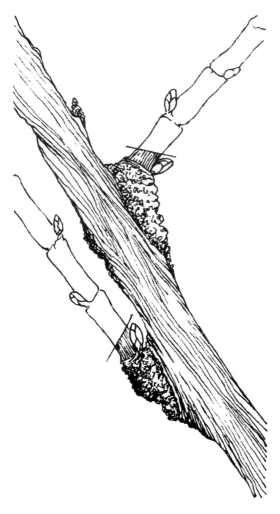

Close-up showing where the fruited canes are cut away from the permanent ones.

When a flower truss has formed, the lateral is normally stopped at two leaves beyond the truss; this varies a little with the variety though. Any side-shoots (sub-laterals) that grow from the fruiting canes should be stopped at one leaf. All tendrils should be removed.

As soon as the initial stopping beyond the flower truss has been done, tie the shoots in to the supporting wires regularly. This has to be done gently so that there are no breakages.

Turning to their outdoor cultivation, vines can perfectly well be grown outside in the southern half of the UK but they do need proper looking after with the right treatment being carried out at the right time of year. With that proviso, there isn't the slightest reason why anyone with a sunny garden shouldn't be very successful.

The decision to make early on is whether you want the grapes for dessert or wine; by and large, the wine varieties don't need as much sunshine as the sweet ones do. As well as the sunshine, we also have to consider the rainfall because all grapes prefer it on the dry side. Anywhere that gets much over 30in (76cm) of rain a year is going to be difficult. Spring frosts can also be troublesome – not so much to the flowers, which don't normally appear until June, but to the tender young shoots. At the other end of the season, early autumn frosts will soon put a stop to the fruit ripening.

Vines are tolerant of a wide range of soils but the warmer sands and gravels usually give the best results. These start the canes into growth early in the year and the drainage is usually good. This is all-important because vines simply won't put up with wet feet Where the quality of the drainage is suspect make sure that the position is properly drained before planting

buds and only the strongest of the two resulting shoots being kept in the spring.

The other pruning time, during the growing season, is necessary to prevent the whole thing getting out of hand and to encourage the vine to produce good grapes. Once the two (or more) shoots from each spur are long enough to see which is the strongest, all others are nipped out.

by digging in plenty of bulky organic matter, such as garden compost or well-rotted manure. A chalky soil doesn't worry them at all – in fact, they rather like it.

If possible, buy and plant one-year-old pot-grown plants and, rather than planting them straight out of the pot, tease the rootball apart and spread out the roots. Plant the roots about 6in (15cm) deep.

The distance between plants will vary according to the method of training chosen. For example, if you intend to have a permanent cane framework trained to a wall or wires, 5ft (1.5m) spaces would be about right. With the Guyot method, though (described later), 3ft (90cm) apart is usually enough.

Although vines are not gross feeders, they certainly need to be looked after if they are to perform well – 4oz of Growmore per square yard in March/April does them proud. On light soils, a good mulch of garden compost or manure can take the place of the Growmore – this helps with water retention and also provides nutrients.

Like all fruits, grapes crop heaviest when pollinated by another variety. They are partially self-fertile, so this isn't vital. They are, however, notoriously bad at setting fruit so are best hand-pollinated.

Training and pruning are probably the most complicated parts of growing vines but even these procedures are really quite easy once you get the hang of them. Because there are several methods of training and pruning, and each has its followers, there's no such thing as 'the best' – outdoors, the Guyot probably comes near the top for all-round ease and efficiency, especially for wine vines.

Following winter planting, the vine is cut down to no more than three buds from the ground. In the first growing season, just one shoot is allowed to develop; all others

are rubbed out as soon as they appear In the winter, this one shoot is cut back to about four buds, the object having been to build up a strong root system.

During the second growing season, the two top buds are allowed to grow out into shoots. As before, all others are rubbed out as they appear From here on each shoot is treated differently, as regards winter pruning. It doesn't matter which shoot you choose, but one must be cut back to two buds. The other is to produce fruiting laterals the following year so is shortened to six buds. It is then bent down and tied to the supporting wire.

During the following (third) growing season, shoots will grow from most of the buds on this cane. These laterals will produce flower trusses and are stopped at two leaves beyond the truss. Any other shoots that appear on them, or on their parent cane, are pinched back to one leaf.

The cane that was reduced to two buds in the winter will send out a shoot from each. These two are allowed to grow unhindered but any others are removed.

In the winter, the laterals that have fruited, together with their parent cane, are removed completely. The other two are treated as were the original two in the previous winter. From then on, simply follow the same routine each year; cutting out the fruited laterals and parent cane and shortening back one of the two others to two buds and the other to six.

The support needed for this Guyot system consists of a horizontal wire 6–8in (15–20cm) from the ground to which will be tied the fruiting cane. You will also need a vertical bamboo to which you tie the two canes as they grow. We can make better use of the space if, instead of just one wire, another is stretched a foot above the first. If the vines are then planted 18in (45cm) apart, instead of the recommended 3ft (90cm), double the crop can be had by training alternate plants to the top wire.

QUINCE AND MEDLAR

Neither fruit is grown widely, but both are perfectly easy. They are interesting and different fruits and have the virtue also of carrying attractive blossoms in the spring. Let us take the quince first.

Quinces

Most of us are familiar with the ornamental shrub 'Japonica'. It has red or orange flowers in the spring, thorns, carries a varying number of fruits the size of a golf ball and is often tied against a fence or wall. This is the ornamental quince, whose correct botanical name is *Chaenomeles*.

The quinces that are grown for their fruits are varieties of *Cydonia oblonga*. In May this has larger white or pink flowers, depending on the variety, followed by hard, pear-like fruits that are ready for picking in late October or November. They cannot be eaten raw.

It makes an attractive tree which will grow perfectly well in the open, but is happier against a warm wall in colder districts. It is thornless, self-fertile and usually starts carrying fruit when five to six years old. The quince does best in a moist and rich soil in a sunny position so that both the fruits and fruit buds ripen properly.

Bush trees in the open garden should be planted 10–12ft(3–3.6m) apart. Those against a wall hardly lend themselves to any particular form of training, but a rough fan shape is probably as good as any.

For the first three to four years all trees should have the branch leaders pruned back in early winter by about half their length to encourage branching. Shoots that are overcrowded are cut back to two or three buds and those that are not in the way can be left to fill up space and to fruit

After about four years no regular pruning will be needed, simply tidying up.

Trees growing on poor soil should be mulched and all should be fed in late winter with 2–4oz (60–120g) of 'Growmore' per sq. yd (m), according to their performance.

Gather the fruits in late October or early November before the frost gets at them and store them away from other fruits or their rather strong and sweet smell can taint apples and pears. Six to eight weeks in the dark is usually enough to mellow them for cooking.

The most commonly grown variety is Vranja from Yugoslavia. It is pear shaped, bright yellow, very fragrant and tender. It grows vigorously and crops at an early age.

Meech's Prolific is another good variety.

The worst affliction of quinces is Leaf Blight which shows itself as spreading reddish patches turning black. Use Bordeaux mixture in June to control it.

Medlars

The other fruit, the medlar, is used for making jelly and is, if possible, even easier to grow. It originally came from the wilds of Asia and Europe, but probably not Britain.

Botanically the medlar is in the rose family and the fruit certainly looks vaguely like a very large rosehip. It is about the size of a golf ball.

The tree growth is somewhat wild and bushy. This makes it difficult to prune in an organised way and, indeed, the best system is to grow it as a bush and only prune it by cutting out shoots and branches to encourage a good shape.

It is rather more of an ornamental tree than a useful one and, on acid land, it can take on a splendid red autumn colour. Beyond this desirability, it has no particular preference as to soil type except that it should never be subject to waterlogging.

The fruit is interesting in that, until it is brown, the flesh is uneatable. Indeed, many people consider it to be uneatable raw even then, but it makes an excellent jelly for eating with meat or game.

Nottingham is the normal and main variety. The fruits are medium sized and the tree crops early in its life.

Another is the Dutch. It is less prolific, but has larger fruit.

KIWI FRUIT

To be honest, and despite what is frequently said and written about them, kiwi fruit are in the same category of hardiness as grapes. If you live in the south, you may be lucky and take a crop off them occasionally, but more often than not, and certainly elsewhere, you will not.

To emphasise this, the only place in the UK where they are grown commercially is in the Channel Isles; and even there they have to be grown in heated greenhouses.

Kiwis need post and wire supports and, if grown outside, provision must be made to protect them from spring frosts and, indeed, from very cold winter weather. Male and female plants have to be grown together to get fruit and, naturally, only the female will carry the fruit. However, there is now a variety, Jenny, that is much handier because the flowers are normal, in that each flower has male and female 'bits'.

Spur pruning is required to keep the plants in check and to encourage fruiting.

Hayward (female) is the most fruitful variety. Tomari (male) is a good pollinator and flowers at the same time.

BLUEBERRIES

These are becoming increasingly popular in this country, both for growing in gardens and simply for buying and eating the fruit.

Botanically, the blueberry is *Vaccinium corymbosum,* a deciduous ericaceous shrub. The heather-like flowers are seen in April/May and are followed by the larger than black currant-sized berries. They are very popular in America.

Their only vice, if such it can be called, is that they require rather strange growing conditions. The soil must always be moist, but at the same time free draining. However, the important point is that it must have a pH in the range of 4–5.5, very acid. These conditions usually prevail in sandy areas, but the snag here is that the sand quickly dries out.

Where soils are only on the borderline of acid, they can be improved by digging in plenty of peat or by dressing the ground with powdered sulphur at 4oz(120g) per sq. yd (m).

On chalky or limey soils, the only answer is to create raised acid borders. The bushes grow to about 5ft (1.5m) and cross-pollination, if not necessary, is desirable. Failing all that, grow the things in large pots containing ericaceous compost. It works a treat.

In the garden, plant the bushes 5ft (1.5m) apart but, if the soil is poor; 4ft (1.2m) is usually enough. Good varieties include Earliblue, Goldtraube, Jersey, Bluecrop, Nui (a new and exceptional variety) and Sunshine Blue (semi-dwarf and also excellent).

Quick Guide to Planting Distances

In most cases a range between two figures is given (e.g. 12–18ft); this takes account of the different vigour of individual varieties and also the quality of the soil.

Apples and Pears

Standards and half-standards	Not less than 18ft(5.5m)
Bush trees	
Semi-vigorous rootstock	12–18ft(3.5–5.5m)
Semi-dwarfing	10–15ft(3–4.5m)
Dwarfing	8–10ft(2.5–3m)
Dwarf pyramids	3–4ft(1–1.25m)
Cordons	2½–3½ft(0.75–1m)
Espaliers	
Dwarfing rootstock	9–12ft(2.7–3.5m)
Semi-dwarfing	12–15ft(3.5–4.5m)
Vigorous	15ft(4.5m)

Plums

Half-standards	18–25ft(5.5–7.5m)
Bush trees	
St Julien A rootstock	15–20ft(4.5–6m)
Pixy	8–10ft(2.5–3m)
Dwarf pyramids	
St Julien A	10–12ft(3–3.5m)
Pixy	6–7ft(approx 2m)
Fan-trained	15–18ft(4.5–5.5m)

Cherries

Half-standard and bush on Colt rootstock 20–25ft(6–7m)
Fan-trained on Colt(allow for 8ft(2.5m) high) 15–18ft(4.5m–5.5m)
Bush or fan-trained on Inmil 8–10ft (2.5–3m)

Peaches, Nectarines and Apricots

Fan-trained on St Julien A rootstock 12–15ft (3.5–4.5m)

Figs

A fan-trained tree should occupy 70–100 sq ft of wall space.

Strawberries

15–18in (40–45cm) between plants; 30–36in (75–90cm) between rows.

Raspberries

Summer varieties   1–2ft(30–60cm) between canes
Autumn varieties   2ft (60cm)

Blackberries

10–15ft (3–4.5m) according to the vigour of the variety. Closest for Ashton Cross, furthest apart for Himalaya Giant and Fantasia.

Hybrid Cane Fruits

Tayberry and loganberry   8ft(2.5m)

Gooseberries

Bush   5ft(1.5cm)
Single cordons   1ft(30cm)
'U' cordons   2ft(60cm)

Red and White Currants

As gooseberries.

Black Currants

Most varieties   5–6ft(1.5–1.8m)
BenSarek   4ft(1.2m)

Further Reading

The *Fruit Garden Displayed*, Harry Baker (RHS)

Soft Fruit Growing, David Turner and Ken Muir (Croom Helm)

The Apple Book, Peter Blackburne-Maze (Collingridge)

Cultivated Fruits of Britain, F. A. Roach (Blackwell)

Apples, John Bultitude (Macmillan Reference Books)

The RHS publishes many relevant and excellent books covering growing fruit at home.

Magazines

Garden News
Garden Answers
Practical Gardening
The Garden (Journal of the RHS)
Amateur Gardening
Kitchen Garden

Useful Addresses

CLUBS AND SOCIETIES

Whilst there are many local horticultural societies and gardening clubs that can be helpful to newcomers to fruit growing, there are very few on a national basis. The benefit of joining a local club is that there could well be members experienced in fruit growing to give you advice; there might also be some who grow fruit commercially.

The best known and most interesting national body is The Fruit Group of the Royal Horticultural Society (RHS). Membership of the group is free but you must already be a member of the RHS. Details can be had from the Secretary of the Fruit Group, Royal Horticultural Society, Vincent Square, London SWIP 2PE.

SUPPLIERS

Nurseries

Many local nurseries and garden centres are able to supply fruit plants of many or most kinds but, more often than not, when a slightly off-beat kind or variety is wanted you draw a blank.

The list of nurseries and fruits given below does not claim to be complete but it includes most kinds of fruit that you are likely to want. These nurseries are not the only ones that will stock a particular kind or variety, but the list includes most of the national specialist growers. The fruits listed under each nursery are those which are carried in a large range of varieties.

Pomona Fruits

PO Box 10618
Walton-on-the Naze
Essex
CO13 3AF
www.pomonafruits.co.uk

M. E. Cook

Keepers Nursery
446 Wateringbury Road
East Mailing
Maidstone
ME19 6JJ

Apples, pears, plums, cherries; especially new varieties.

Deacon's Nursery

Moor View
Godshill
Isle of Wight
PO38 3HW
www.deaconsnurseryfruits.co.uk

Apples, apricots, cherries, nuts, peaches and nectarines, pears, plums and cane fruits.

Highfield Nurseries

School Lane
Whitminster
Gloucester
GL2 7PL
www.highfield-nurseries.co.uk

Fairly general.

Scott's Nurseries Ltd

Higher Street
Merriott
Somerset
TA16 5PL

Apples, cherries, gooseberries, peaches and nectarines, pears, plums, quinces.

J. Tweedie

Fruit Tree Nursery
504 Denby Dale Road West
Calder Grove
Wakefield
WF4 3DB

Maryfield Road Nursery
Terregles
Dumfries
DG2 9TH

Apples, black currants, cherries, gooseberries, peaches and nectarines.

Read's Nursery

Hales Hall
Lodden
Norfolk
NRI4 6QW

The leading specialist in exotic and greenhouse fruits.

Adam's Apples

Egremont Barn
Payhembury
Honiton
Devon
EX14 3JA
www.adamsappletrees.co.uk

Ashridge Trees

Grove Cross Barn
Grove Cross
Castle Cary
Somerset
BA7 7NJ
www.ashridgetrees.co.uk

Bernwode Fruit Trees

Kingswood Lane
Ludgershall
Buckinghamshire
HP18 9RB
www.bernwodeplants.co.uk

Blackmoor Nurseries

Blackmoor
Nr Liss
Hampshire
GU33 6BS
www.blackmoor.co.uk

Cornish Apple Trees

www.cornishappletrees.co.uk

Keepers Nursery

Gallants Court
East Farleigh
Maidstone
Kent
ME15 0LE
www.keepers-nursery.co.uk

Buckingham Nurseries

Tingewick Road
Buckingham
MK18 4AE
www. buckingham-nurseries.co.uk

Ornamental Tree Nurseries

Cobnash
Kingsland
Herefordshire
HR6 9QZ
www.ornamental-trees.co.uk

Suffolk Fruit and Trees

The Orchards
Oaktree House
Braiseworth near Eye
Suffolk
IP23 7DS
www.realenglishfruit.co.uk

As a general rule, it is advisable, but not essential, to buy outdoor plants from a supplier in your own area. They have probably been raised locally and will, therefore, be accustomed to your climate.

Avoid the temptation of buying from a nursery in a colder locality than your own. There used to be a belief that it would mean stronger plants in your milder area. The result is usually increased vigour, leading to larger trees and, consequently, lighter crops.

CATALOGUES

The following all supply fruit seeds, plants and garden equipment, available to buy online or by mail order catalogue.

D.T. Brown
Bury Road
Newmarket
CB8 7PQ
www.dtbrownseeds.co.uk

Samuel Dobie & Son
Long Road
Paignton
Devon
TQ4 7SX
www.dobies.co.uk

Mr Fothergill's
Kentford
Suffolk
CB8 7QB
www.mr-fothergills.co.uk

Kings Seeds
Monks Farm
Kelvedon
Colchester
Essex
CO5 9PG
www.kingsseeds.com

Marshalls Seeds
Alconbury Hill
Huntingdon
Cambs
PE28 4HY
www. marshalls-seeds.co.uk

Moles Seeds (UK) Ltd
Turkey Cock Lane
Stanway
Colchester
Essex
CO3 8PD
www.molesseeds.co.uk

Orange Pippin Ltd
www. orangepippin.com

The Organic Gardening Catalogue
Riverdene Business Park
Molesey Road
Hersham
Surrey
KT12 4RG
www.organiccatalog.com

J. Parker
14 Hadfield Street
Old Trafford
Manchester
M16 9FG
www.jparkers.co.uk

Seeds of Italy Ltd
A1 Phoenix Industrial Estate
Rosslyn Crescent
Harrow
Middlesex
HA1 2SP
www.seedsofitaly.com

Suttons Seeds
Woodview Road
Paignton
Devon
TQ4 7NG
www.suttons.co.uk

Thompson and Morgan
Poplar Lane
Ipswich
Suffolk
IP8 3BU
www.thompson-morgan.com

Urban Allotments
Hope Valley Meadows
Minsterley
Shropshire
SY5 0JX
www. urban-allotmments.com

Unwins Seeds
www.unwins.co.uk

GARDENING EQUIPMENT

Hoses and Irrigation Equipment

Hozelock-ASL Ltd
Haddenham
Aylesbury
Buckinghamshire
HP17 8JD

Spray Chemicals and Weedkillers

The Scotts Co. Ltd.
Salisbury House
Weyside Park
Godalming
Surrey
GU7 1XE

Bayer Garden
230 Cambridge Science Park
Milton Road
Cambridge
CB4 0WB

Sprayers

Hozelock Sprayers Ltd.
Midpoint Park
Birmingham
B76 1AB

Pruning Equipment

Burton McCall Ltd.
163 Parker Drive
Leicester
LE4 0JP

GREENHOUSES

Hall's Greenhouses
211 Chester Road
New Oscott
Sutton Coldfield
B73 5BD
www.hallsgreenhouses.co.uk

Hall's Greenhouses
209 Chester Road
Castle Bromwich
Birmingham
B36 0ET
www.hallsgreenhouses.co.uk

Gabriel Ash
Monument Farm
Farndon
Chester
CH3 6QP
www.gabrielash.com

Alton Greenhouses
Station Works
Fenny Compton
Southam
Warwickshire
CV47 2XB
www.altongreenhouses.co.uk

Index

Other Gardening Books from Crowood

Cunningham, Sally, *Ecological Gardening*
Gray, Linda, *Herb Gardening*
Gregson, Sally, *Ornamental Vegetable Gardening*
Gregson, Sally, *Practical Propagation*
Hodge, Geoff, *Pruning*
Jones, Peter, *Gardening on Clay*
Littlewood, Michael, *The Organic Gardener's Handbook*
Marder, John, *Water-Efficient Gardening*
Nottridge, Rhoda, *Wildlife Gardening*
Saunders, Bridgette, *Allotment Gardening*